D0981256

Notching Up

the NURTURED HEART APPROACH
The New Inner Wealth Initiative
for Educators

Notching Up

the NURTURED HEART APPROACH
The New Inner Wealth Initiative
for Educators

by Howard Glasser with Melissa Lynn Block

the NURTURED HEART APPROACH
The New Inner Wealth Initiative
for Educators

Copyright 2011 by Howard Glasser with Melissa Lynn Block

For information contact: Nurtured Heart Publications
4165 West Ironwood Hill Drive
Tucson, Arizona 85745
E-mail: adhddoc@theriver.com

For information about bulk purchasing discounts of this book or other Nurtured Heart Approach books, videos, CDs or DVDs, please contact Fulfillment Services at 800-311-3132. For orders within the book industry, please contact Brigham Distributing at 435-723-6611.

Heart paintings by Anne Labovitz
Book design by Richard Diffenderfer
Back cover design idea by Alice Glasser
Copy editing by Chris Howell
Printed by Pollock Printing, Nashville, TN

Library of Congress Card Catalogue Number: Pending
ISBN 978-0-9826714-2-9
First Edition: January 2011 - Printed in the United States
Second Edition: September 2013 - Printed in China

*This book is dedicated to educators who are determined
to cultivate the greatness of their students.
You are transforming not only individual lives,
but also families, schools and communities.*

*In so doing, you participate in transporting humanity
into an age where greatness is a guiding force.*

The greatness in me sees the greatness in you!

Table of Contents

Why a New Nurtured Heart Approach Book for Educators?

THIS BOOK IS A SEQUEL to *The Inner Wealth Initiative: the Nurtured Heart Approach for Educators,* which has been used as a resource by teachers, school counselors and administrators since 2007.

Why a new book for educators? As often happens when a practice expands from being applied by two or three or ten people to use by hundreds or thousands, the Nurtured Heart Approach has evolved since it was first conceived in the early 1990s. Over the years, I have seen the approach I created being applied with ingenuity by many amazing people, which is a true honor and privilege for me. Along with the widespread interest in this body of work comes a commensurate risk, however: that this evolution could progress to places that, for me, do not jive with the approach's core principles.

As the approach's creator, I wanted to return to the foundations of the method to clarify them as well as to avoid any misunderstandings about the method that might have arisen over the years of its practice.

Since its beginnings, the Nurtured Heart Approach has revealed itself to be more than a set of techniques for adults who wish to manage children's behavior: *Children are transformed as a result of the approach's effect on the outlook and actions of the adult.*

This approach isn't about creating improvements in problem kids or managing behavior. It's about creating a transformation *in adults* that is founded in a belief in the inherent greatness of all children. For many of us, making this happen for children entails awakening or renewing our belief that this greatness exists in every person—ourselves included! In this new book, this notion is taken further than it is in my previous book for educators.

The original book certainly contains the fundamentals, but its main thrust is to teach through application, anecdotes and a lot of "What if?" questions. ("What if a child does this? Or this? Or this?") These were designed to help teachers prepare themselves for every possible eventuality. However, two things became evident soon after the original book for schools went into widespread use:

- I could never begin to illuminate all the possible scenarios a teacher might encounter. They're endless!

- By its nature, this very design creates a dependency. It never quite gets the educator to true independence—the point where the teacher knows the approach so well that she can respond to every possible situation and answer all of her own burning questions. She has a deep enough sense of the approach to adjust its foundational pieces to work in any scenario.

1

Techniques, anecdotes and "what if" examples can and do propel transformation. But a more direct way is to support the educator in making an *internal* shift to a new 'default setting' where inadvertent negativity shifts into a positivity that fully supports greatness. Accomplishing this shift is the primary focus of this book.

Instead of searching a book's pages trying to find the particular example to address a current dilemma or show you the path to take when things go wrong, you will become progressively aligned with the core of this method at an internal level. For teachers who struggle with integrating (or finding the right balance between) the many techniques and approaches in which they have been trained, I hope to offer a new core direction that ends the need to cobble together pieces of other approaches to classroom management and character education. I hope to provide more than a "how-to" approach to keeping your classroom under control—rather, I present a body of work and philosophy compelling enough to inspire new direction and clarity in your work and in other aspects of your life.

My hope is that this new book for educators will bring about a shift to positivity at the level of the 'primary' brain—the part of the brain that ordinarily jumps to fear, worry and doubt and that almost always expects the worst. This book is a guide to a way of thinking and a practice that acknowledges this habitual tendency toward negativity…and then purposefully shifts from that tendency to one of cultivating greatness.

Any educator who has dealt with difficult students and out-of-control classrooms (not to mention the many other burdens faced by educators that have little to do with student behavior) is likely to be intimately acquainted with a fear-based way of thinking. Educators who learn the approach from this book will learn to 'flip a switch' that assures the fight-or-flight brain that it can handle any school situation by applying this approach at ever deeper and more gratifying levels.

This new book for educators reflects my faith that the reader can, through a deeper shift of intention into what I call the *greatness mindset*, create his or her very own journey into greatness. This is the journey I've been on for some years now, and it is truly awesome. It has given me the tools to handle any situation the universe throws at me. And I've seen what this shift to the greatness mindset in educators can do to transform individuals, families, counseling practices, classrooms and whole schools. In addition to making the concepts and techniques of the approach more crystal clear than ever, we hope to show how you can explore and expand your own greatness…and the greatness of all the children whose lives you impact.

Here's to *your* greatness!

—*Howard Glasser*

Foreword

BY Michael Gilbert, Psy.D.

A REVOLUTION IS UNDERWAY in communities across the country to transform children to a greater level of success, well-being and achievement. At the center of this movement is the Nurtured Heart Approach, a social-emotional curriculum developed by Howard Glasser.

Today's predominant educational and mental health systems are failing a large number of our children. Educational data continue to clearly demonstrate that what we are doing is simply not working. Our agenda has become largely about controlling children's behavior, managing classrooms and teaching to meaningless tests. Dropout and graduation rates are at unacceptable levels, students are under-achieving and negativity has become an expected part of the school environment.

Students we can't control get referred to other failing systems, such as special education or mental health. Our traditional mental health system continues to label more children, label them at younger ages, prescribe more harmful medications and increasingly engage in polypharmacy (i.e., more than one medication). Despite the lack of evidence to support the 'medical model' or the long-term efficacy of psychiatric medications, we continue on the same path.

Look closely at the operations of these systems and you will notice that they are constantly in crisis. Reform efforts frequently fail. Attempts at change are often derailed by administrative bureaucracy. Many programs only address deep concerns on a superficial level.

What do we really want for our children? Most would agree that our intention should be to assist students in developing strong character, inner strength, resiliency, self-control, purpose and self-confidence. We need to accept that traditional approaches have not had the desired effect and recognize that we, as educators, parents and counselors to children, possess the capacity to inspire all children to flourish and express their intelligence, intensity and creativity in amazing ways. To transform failing systems, we need to abandon our misconceptions about what motivates children—misconceptions on which traditional approaches are built. Then, we need to create classroom and school communities that foster a student's intrinsic motivation to make positive choices throughout the day. The Nurtured Heart Approach is designed to create exactly this kind of intrinsic positive motivation in both students and educators.

In order to make a significant impact on the well-being of children in our educational and mental health systems, we must adopt a new aim: that of

3

transforming relationships between children and educators. To this end, our mission in education should be to establish social and emotional learning (SEL) as a critical component of the school community. Despite the fact that many SEL programs currently in use produce some positive, albeit modest changes, they do not get to the core of the individual child like the Nurtured Heart Approach (NHA).

Currently, NHA is being utilized in classrooms and school districts across the country as well as internationally. Evidence is being gathered that illustrates improved academics, a decrease in negative behavior, a reduction in referrals to special education and mental health, an increase in academic engagement, and reduced teacher attrition. More importantly, students are experiencing a transformation that will lead them to become life-long learners who are caring, responsible, self-aware and determined.

The Nurtured Heart Approach is not just another positive approach that sits on a shelf only to occasionally be taken down for a 10-minute lesson on desirable values like respect or responsibility. Instead, the Nurtured Heart Approach is the scaffolding on which meaningful relationships are built. The approach is used throughout the day and across settings and is equally important in the interactions among staff as it is between teachers and students. Teachers and other adults 'become the approach,' and eventually it becomes a natural part of everyday life.

The NHA should be a foundation in our educational settings. As part of the tiered model currently being utilized in schools, it needs to be at the tier-one (i.e., universal) level. This translates to all staff creating opportunities for nurturing and responsive relationship with students, which has been shown to be pivotal to a child's development. The approach also produces language-enriched interactions, which build student vocabulary. And ultimately, the approach leads to much more: great character.

Imagine a world where families, schools and communities work together to promote children's ultimate success in school and life. We can change the life of a child, a classroom, a community—and yes, we can change the world. The ripples are already in motion. This book will guide you to a shift in perspective via the inner wealth that already exists within you and the fearlessness to become an agent of change.

Inspire greatness!

Dr. Gilbert has worked in the human services field for over 20 years, including foster care, group home and hospital settings, as a school psychologist in the Syracuse (NY) City Schools for the past 12 years, as well as an adjunct professor at local colleges. In 2000, he founded It's About Childhood & Family, Inc., a not-for-profit clinic and resource center, and recently launched the Inner Wealth Initiative in Central New York as a grassroots movement designed to provide families an alternative to the traditional mental health system. He has given presentations to parents and professionals throughout New York State as well as nationally. Currently, he is conducting research evaluating non-medication approaches for families and teachers with children exhibiting challenging behaviors, commonly diagnosed as Attention Deficit Hyperactive Disorder, Oppositional Defiant Disorder or Bipolar Disorder. Dr. Gilbert is on the Board of Directors for the International Center for the Study of Psychiatry and Psychology as well as the annual conference chairperson.

Acknowledgments

I AM INFINITELY GRATEFUL to all those who've danced the Nurtured Heart Approach out to the world in so many brilliant ways. I've been awed by their great intention to nurture the hearts of the children of this world.

I am overwhelmingly appreciative of Melissa Lynn Block. She is so adept at giving wings to my voice and thoughts as well as expressing the brilliance of her experiences and inspiration as a Nurtured Heart Approach Advanced Trainer and parent. She is an amazing force; she possesses the greatness of relentlessly moving the ball downfield toward the goal! That determination, zeal and brilliance are precious qualities of greatness. She made this project an absolute pleasure at every stage.

I am so grateful to Lisa Bravo, who constantly keeps me inspired, laughing and in gear—and who is collaborating with Melissa on the companion workbook to this volume.

To the Advanced Trainers who offered their inspiring stories, many of which were woven into this book: Celeste Elsey, Stephanie Rule, Karen Calkins, Pat Bethke, Dan Petersen, Tammy Jacobs and Tammy Small. Thank you so much for the great work you are doing.

Thank you to the 'Greatness Kids' at Cooley Middle School for showing me what is possible.

I certainly must thank the members of my editorial and design team, without whom a work like this would not be possible. Chris Howell has now edited nine Nurtured Heart books, and each and every time has impressed me more with her nurturing, thorough approach as she guides the manuscript through its process of being born. Chris, I applaud the greatness of your wonderful leadership on this project. Also, great appreciation to Richard Diffenderfer, who seamlessly, gracefully, calmly and coolly provided the graphic touches to bring the manuscript to print-ready book form. Rich, your brilliance is so greatly appreciated.

Lastly, I wish to thank the two artists in my life: my daughter Alice, for ongoing inspiration and proof that this approach results in a life of greatness; and our new Nurtured Heart Approach Advanced Trainer and greatness artist Anne Labovitz for her inspiring and beautiful cover art.

—*Howard Glasser*

Collaborating with Howard Glasser is an honor and a pleasure. I'm immeasurably thankful that he and his approach came into my life when my children were very young. It has made me a better parent and a more joyous, positive person. And now that we've worked together so much for so long, co-creating with him is hardly like work—it feels more like a fast-paced, engaging dance! And being involved with the approach and becoming an Advanced Trainer has brought so many fascinating, dedicated people into my life. The Nurtured Heart community is really special, and I feel privileged to be part of it.

My children, Sarah and Noah, and my step-children, Julian and Tristan, are constant inspirations and supports to me. So are Amanda, Nicola, Sumati, Robin, Misa, Katie, Elizabeth, Jacque, Anya, Peggy, Barbara, and the rest of my happily expanding tribe of strong woman friends. Thanks also to my wonderful community at the Unitarian Society of Santa Barbara, where I've taught this approach to many parents; to my mom, dad, sister and brother; and to Patrick, with whom I continue to grow and explore.

—*Melissa Lynn Block*

About the Authors

HOWARD GLASSER is the founder of the Children's Success Foundation and creator of the Nurtured Heart Approach, which has been used in hundreds of thousands of homes and classrooms around the world.

He is author of *Transforming the Difficult Child*, currently the top-selling book on the topic of ADHD; *The Inner Wealth Initiative*, one of the leading books on school interventions; *You Are Oprah – Igniting the Fires of Greatness*, a book that outlines ways to apply the Nurtured Heart Approach to one's self; and *All Children Flourishing*, a book that describes the approach's use with all children, difficult or not. Four of his eight books are in the top one percent of all books on Amazon.com.

Howard has been a featured guest on CNN and a consultant for *48 Hours*. He currently teaches the Nurtured Heart Approach through live presentations worldwide. He is former director of the Center for the Difficult Child in Tucson, Arizona, and has been a consultant for numerous psychiatric, judicial and educational programs. Although he has done extensive doctoral work in the fields of clinical psychology and educational leadership, he feels his own years as an intense and challenging child contributed the most to his understanding of the needs of these children and to the strength of his approach.

His work is being successfully applied across programs from in-home family therapy to residential treatment; from varied areas of foster care to all areas of mental health treatment; from marital counseling for troubled relationships to helping couples relate in greatness; from substance abuse treatment to programs for the returning military and gang members; from fostering inner wealth in infants and toddlers to eldercare programs; and in the education field, in settings ranging from Head Start to high schools to special education.

Howard has been called one of the most influential living persons working to prevent children from needing psychiatric medications. His work has also supported many children in developing the inner strength to choose against addictive substances.

He resides in Tucson and has one daughter, Alice, a gifted artist who has created covers for four of his books.

MELISSA LYNN BLOCK is a writer and editor who has authored, co-authored and ghostwritten over 25 books in addition to countless articles, newsletters, blog postings, short stories and poetry.

She is also a yoga teacher, nutrition and fitness expert, visual artist, contemporary dancer and choreographer, and devoted mother of two children, Sarah and Noah. She became a Nurtured Heart Approach Advanced Trainer in 2009 and has since taught several classes in the approach. In 2010, she assisted Howard in teaching the first online course in the approach.

Melissa can be contacted at ideokinesis.mlb@gmail.com.

Cover art by Anne Labovitz

ANNE LABOVITZ earned a degree in art and art history from Hamline University in Saint Paul, Minnesota, in 1989. She has lived and worked in Switzerland, Germany, Spain and Italy and currently lives in Saint Paul, Minnesota. A painter and printmaker, she specializes in portraiture and expressive colored abstracts. From childhood, color has provided deep inspiration for her and continues to powerfully inform her work. Her work is held in collections in the United States and Europe. Anne also happens to be an advanced Nurtured Heart trainer.

Her 'Loving Heart' series of paintings began as a commission done on a large scale but over time she produced them on a smaller scale and with a more intimate feel. These hearts are directly inspired by the Nurtured Heart Approach. Anne states: "I have created these paintings through the act of listening to and digesting the Nurtured Heart Approach, enabling me to dial into the core of this work. The inspiration expresses itself in the form of a healing heart. I conceived these paintings joyfully in acrylic paint on canvas." The originals are 12 by 12 inches. Anne's work can be viewed at www.labovitz.com.

Preface

The Hidden Curriculum

FEW PEOPLE ARE AS MEANINGFUL to a young person as a teacher. No other social environment outside the home is more encompassing or important than school. A child's school experience can elevate him or her above all obstacles.

In college, teachers-in-the-making learn all sorts of effective methods for teaching facts and conveying knowledge. Far fewer strategies are imparted regarding how to teach a love of learning or how to cultivate open-mindedness, fluidity of thought or an appreciation of differing points of view. Teachers learn even fewer effective strategies for teaching students to achieve self-love and a sense of their own greatness. But when school is just a distant memory, students will remember—far more clearly than facts, figures and projects—the teachers who inspired them, who made school a relevant and rewarding force in their lives, and perhaps most importantly, who fostered in them a belief in and love of themselves.

This non-academic curriculum for which you, the educator, are at least partially responsible is sometimes called the *hidden curriculum*. If you're an educator, you already know that this hidden curriculum is, in part, about values, self-esteem and relationships. It teaches students that:

- they belong in the adventure of life;
- they are meaningful and valued;
- their actions create a response from the world around them; and
- they can believe in themselves.

This hidden curriculum also teaches students crucial lessons on how to:

- access their resilience and strengths;
- treat one another and move through the world;
- communicate with others;
- be open to life; and
- make the most of their growing sense of self.

In classrooms where academic curriculum is king—where educators shoulder the heavy burden of ill-conceived government programs that ultimately leave every other child behind—these important aspects of education tend to fall by the wayside.

Even as classrooms become populated with more intense and demanding children, hope remains that educators will be able to impart some of these aspects of the hidden curriculum to students. The good news is that, with every interaction between adults and children—indeed, in any interaction involving adults that is witnessed by a child—we teach this hidden curriculum, whether we mean to or not. We don't have to *try* to teach it. Children are watching like hawks for information about how to be and how to live, and they download the basic forms and formats mostly through observation of the adults in their lives, beginning at birth. This happens below the spoken level, at the level of energetic exchange.

If we do not *intentionally* bring a positive and uplifting form of this curriculum to children during our interactions with them, they'll learn from whatever we *do* bring. And most teachers, through no fault of their own, end up unintentionally teaching a version of the hidden curriculum that they wouldn't dream of teaching if they were aware of an alternative. This book is about a conscious, intentional approach to the hidden curriculum called the Nurtured Heart Approach.

Nurtured Heart is an approach that turns traditional modes of discipline and character education upside-down. At first as you learn it, you may find that it feels strange, even wrong. I have had the experience, probably thousands of times, of seeing people flounder a bit, then "get it." As the dots connect, they start to say things like, "That makes perfect sense!" Or "This seemed so upside-down to me at first, but now I see that it's actually *right-side-up!*" That 'aha moment' is the beginning of a transformation in your way of communicating with and teaching the children in your life.

Nurtured Heart is an approach to *radical appreciation* that compels students at a soul level to live in their greatness. It teaches the hidden curriculum through imparting and inspiring great values, choices, relationship skills and wisdom.

If putting out disciplinary fires and dealing with bureaucratic complexities have made you wonder whether you ought to choose a new profession, don't draft that letter of resignation yet. If you want to take control of your classroom back from difficult students and if you're looking for a way to steer all kids to genuinely *want* to follow the rules and live out their greatness—this approach is for you.

Introduction

The 'Greatness Kids'

ON A BLUSTERY DAY late in October 2009, I stood in a middle-school library in Placer County, California, surrounded by about 120 kids. They belonged to a group of students who had, through a peer mentoring and leadership program, learned the Nurtured Heart Approach.

Their principal, Karen Calkins, called them the "greatness kids," and as I stood in front of those brilliant young souls, all of whom looked genuinely excited to meet me, I found it difficult to speak. More than that: I had an up-surging of emotion so powerful that tears came. The whole notion of kids learning this approach and using it to support and promote success in their classmates stirred my imagination and thrilled me to the core. When I found my voice— it took a minute, and the kids waited patiently—I told them the truth of that moment: "I don't know if I've ever been so honored."

I thought back to a day a few years earlier when I had been in my office, laughing hysterically while watching a video clip. My then-middle-school-aged daughter Alice had come to see what all the ruckus was about. "It's a clip someone sent me of Robin Williams talking about golf," I told her, trying to regain my composure. "Can I see it?" she asked. "I'd love to show it to you," I answered, "but I can't…it's filled with four-letter words." She calmly replied, "*Dad*…in middle school, every other word is a four-letter word!"

Middle school can be ground zero for four-letter words, acting out, bullying, meanness, cliques and peer pressure. And these kids were choosing to act out *greatness* instead.

As the students and I talked about "confronting" each other with greatness, I saw that these kids had a much broader and deeper understanding of this word than most. We weren't talking about greatness in the way it's used in standard conversation, where the word "great" is tossed around without much thought or sincerity behind it. They had been taught by their teachers to see greatness in a new, expansive light.

If you have ever felt awe, wonder and profound appreciation in the face of all of the beauty and grace that surrounds us, you won't have any trouble understanding this more expansive definition of *greatness* as used in this book. Awe, wonder and appreciation are all qualities of greatness. If you see that each being who walks the planet is a microcosm of that more universal greatness, you are on the cusp of accepting that every child in your classroom has inherent greatness, as do you. The approach described in this book will teach you how to identify, access, describe and cultivate, in loving detail, the various qualities of that greatness.

At Cooley Middle School that day, kids demonstrated that they had developed this skill by 'picking on' other kids who volunteered: picking on their *greatness*, that is. Energizing positive reflections began to ricochet around the room. "He doesn't talk behind your back. He's really nice and considerate—he doesn't say anything negative," one boy said of his friend. I asked the group, "What's positive about *him* that he can see this in his friend?" Several in the group answered: "He's thoughtful." "He's loyal." "He doesn't gossip either."

"Have you met someone who isn't thoughtful?" I asked them. They all had (surprise, surprise). "We all know how *not* great it is when someone isn't thoughtful. So it's truly great that these two are so thoughtful, isn't it?" Nodding of heads and quiet agreement. "How many of you like being around positive people?" I asked, and there was a huge show of hands.

Math and leadership teacher Cari Prater chimed in with: "You're showing amazing character by standing up before your peers to be recognized. Many school cultures would ridicule this."

These students were part of a program called E-period (E for "Excel"). During one class period four times a week, they served as mentors and helpers to students who were falling behind academically. They had been taught the Nurtured Heart Approach in preparation for taking on a mentorship role with their peers. As the dialogue with me continued, the students asked questions about how to better use the approach. One wanted to know how to deal with peers who didn't seem open to their support. Another asked, "What do you think are the best traits for a mentor?" Instead of responding myself, I asked the group to answer. Adults and students offered these traits: collaboration, cooperation, authenticity, caring and helpfulness. Another student asked how to get a group of kids to focus on their schoolwork during E-period. Special education teacher Celeste Elsey answered that one. "Focus on one kid who's following the rules and really hone in. Let others see you giving him your attention and appreciation. And," she added, "I want to energize you for your amazing eye contact—you're showing such composure right now, looking right into my eyes as I answer your question. That's star quality!"

As we wrapped up, I thanked the students for handling my earlier show of emotion so well. "You supported me. I felt your kindness. These are qualities of your greatness." They graciously accepted my reflection of them as supportive, kind people. This all made perfect sense to them. It was one of the most fulfilling experiences I've had speaking to a group—and I've spoken to hundreds of groups.

Following this session with the students, a small group of adults gathered in one of the offices: my co-author Melissa, principal Karen Calkins, Celeste Elsey, school psychologist Mary Martin, and ex-school counselor Stephanie Rule (who had taken leave from Cooley to care for the seventh person in the room, five-month-old baby Josilyn).

The teachers who work for Karen obviously adore her. Equally obvious was the respect and adoration of every student who crossed her path while I was there.

"She was doing Nurtured Heart before we even knew it existed!" Mary told the group. "She has always given huge recognitions to staff." Celeste agreed, recalling her first evaluation meeting in her new job at Cooley: "I knew everything I'd done wrong, and I was cringing, waiting to be called out. And in that evaluation, Karen did not say a single negative thing. I heard only about what I had done right!" Melissa added, "You already knew what you had done wrong, anyway." "Exactly," said Karen, "wrong is a waste of time."

The Nurtured Heart Approach found its way into Cooley Middle School in the usual way. School psychologist Mary, who daily had endured challenges with the most difficult students, saw a flyer advertising a training seminar on the approach but tossed it in the trash. When another flyer showed up later on, she decided to take it home and go online to see what it was about. She thought it seemed potentially valuable, but there was no money in the school's budget to send anyone to the training. Somehow, Karen scraped together the needed funds and sent Stephanie to the one-day training. Celeste and Mary were able to go, too, because the district office paid for them to attend.

"When I first talked to Karen about this training, she bought it hook, line and sinker," Stephanie told the group. "She said, 'You're going! I don't care if there's no money! This is *exactly* what Cooley needs!'" Karen was next to go to a training, and in the fall of 2008, all staff members were trained in the approach. Mary, Celeste and Stephanie ultimately became advanced trainers via the week-long training I offer each year in my home city of Tucson.

As the approach has spread throughout the school, there's a prevailing respect for it, but not every teacher practices it. Some even joked about it—including Cari Prater, who has since become one of its fiercest proponents and who has committed herself to getting more teachers on board. "We're not mandating use of the approach," Karen told me, "but if a teacher comes to me saying he or she has tried everything under the sun with a difficult child and nothing is working, I'm going to suggest the Nurtured Heart Approach."

So: What is this approach that has stirred up excitement in all of these wonderful educators and students? It was not created through rigorous large-scale educational research, nor was it created based on any approach that came before it. It was born from my frustration over the lack of positive impact I was having in my role as a therapist treating difficult children. I actually like to say that *it* created *me*.

Chapter 1

The Birth of the Nurtured Heart Approach

AFTER COMPLETING MY DEGREE IN PSYCHOLOGY, I went into practice doing a form of treatment with adults called milieu therapy. I had studied with the people who birthed that movement and had loved being a part of it. Then I took 10 years away from being a therapist to follow my dream of doing wood-working and sculpture. When I returned to work as a therapist, family therapy seemed like the best fit for me.

There I was, in a clinical setting, with a steady flow of clients. I was giving the best advice I knew how to give. I had read all the right books and had taken classes at the highest level. But I began to clearly see that my advice was actually *making things worse*. This clarity may have been due to the fact that I had been away from therapy for a while and had fresh eyes, but I had no doubt that I was *not* helping these families.

So, what did I do? I amped up my advice. I went searching for new strategies that might push what I'd already learned to the level needed. I tried to notch it up. Lo and behold: I found that my enhanced efforts were multiplying the damage and complications these families were facing. I was supposed to be helping, but instead, I was contributing to the demise of families.

I could have walked away, but I hung in there long enough for something odd to happen. Spontaneously, I began to experience an almost molecular recollection of my own life as an exquisitely difficult child.

My own intensity as a child and the emotions I had been embroiled in during those years kept flooding my consciousness. I could feel, viscerally and deeply, many memories and sensations I had tried to forget, especially in relation to family dynamics. This coincided with a period of time where I couldn't quiet down even for a moment without being struck by strange insights and epiphanies. My internal message system kept chiming, "You've got mail!"

These insights seemed, at the outset, too silly to even share with another human being, much less utilize in my therapy practice. I was able to actually *see* the exchange of energy that went on between people—between me and my clients, and between parents and their children. This energetic exchange revealed to me the reasons why my old methods weren't working, and how I might change what I was doing with challenging children in order to actually have the impact I wanted to have—namely, to have a healing effect on children who might otherwise end up diagnosed and drugged.

I'm not sure whether it was intuition, channeling or transmissions from another dimension or another planet, but I listened and began taking action. Reluctantly, tentatively, I started to integrate these notions into my work with parents of difficult children who were coming to me for help. I was amazed by the immediate positive reaction I saw in the families.

The response from parents was consistently: "Ohhh, YES, that makes total sense!" As I refined these notions into strategies, I began to have the inspiring effect that had eluded me before. What I was doing worked so well that referrals began to flood in. My phone started ringing off the hook. "You're walking on water," fellow clinicians told me. "Word on the street is you can cure kids with ADHD." I found myself treating increasingly difficult children: street kids, kids in and out of shelters, gang kids, drug-involved kids, kids who were housed in psychiatric treatment centers, juvenile delinquents…in other words, the toughest kids in town.

As I saw the amazing results of this new approach for these intense children (ultimately called the Nurtured Heart Approach), I came to a realization about ADHD. The truth is that I don't believe in ADHD even though my first book, *Transforming the Difficult Child,* is often said to be the top-selling book on ADHD.

Yes, there are symptoms that have come to be labeled as such. I know that adults tear their hair out in anguish, frustration and fear over children who are annoying, challenging, out of control, or even a threat to their own safety and the safety of others. Millions of kids express disruptiveness, impulsivity, aggression and under-functioning. But I do not choose to label this by giving it a diagnosis, because I have seen some of the most challenging children—almost all the difficult children I've encountered professionally, including children who were 'textbook' ADHD according to the current diagnostic criteria—transformed over the course of only a few weeks. *The intensity that once drove adults to distraction becomes the driving force behind these children's greatness.*

How is this achieved? The adults in their lives are given the tools they require to be the child's therapist—therapist simply means "agent of change"—and the child correspondingly learns to live his or her life in a stunning way, with commitment to self, others and with great intention. If this is possible with an approach that doesn't involve the use of psychotropic drugs, can we say that this child had a brain disorder to start with? My belief is that previous approaches simply haven't been right for these kids.

Case in point: the story of Cooley Middle School student Sean, who had been difficult since *before birth*; his mother, Anna, was on bed rest for six months of her pregnancy due to strong premature labor. Before birth and through his first year, Sean seemed unusually active. He lacked any sense of focus and made minimal eye contact. A visit to a pediatric neurologist ruled out autism but led to an ADHD diagnosis. As Sean grew older, he developed strong obsessive-compulsive tendencies and engaged in unpredictable and sometimes dangerous behaviors. At age four, for example, he shoved his younger brother down a long staircase to see whether his Robin costume would enable him to fly.

School psychologist Mary Martin shared with me that, before his parents discovered the Nurtured Heart Approach, Sean "had no friends, was bullied by others, had no concept of rejection and no social skills." He also had significant sleep problems and was argumentative at home, especially with his younger brother. Sean's academic difficulties were substantial, too, despite having a high-average intelligence level. His poor grades were due to lack of organizational skills and difficulty turning in assignments.

There were more visits to pediatric physicians and psychologists, all of whom seemed eager to try new medications. "We became quasi-pharmacists, Googling medications and investigating camps, treatment centers, books, you name it," his mother Anna told me. They read every book published about ADHD and joined national support groups; tried special diets; tested for apnea at an overnight medical facility; tried holistic medicines; had allergy testing done; and attended behavior modification counseling sessions. "And all of that was good," Anna told me. "We never once regretted gaining knowledge and continuing to learn." A diagnosis of Asperger's syndrome (a form of autism) was eventually added to Sean's other diagnoses.

The years passed, and for Anna and her husband Todd, both busy professionals who eventually had two additional children to care for, it felt like a full-time job just to keep their eldest son in mainstream classrooms. There were many parent-teacher conferences, 504 plans, and much love and kindness from teachers and administrators.

Sean's disruptive behavior tended to worsen in spring, and the spring of 2009 followed suit. As he began to enter puberty, his behavior worsened exponentially; he was constantly angry and hateful. Before this, he had sometimes been tender and loving, and his parents missed this terribly. "One morning, by chance or intervention from above, I wandered into the office of Mary Martin, our loving district psychologist," Anna said. "Mary had evaluated Sean for his 504 plan and knew our situation well. I confided that we were at our wits' end—we couldn't live the way we had been living, and we felt helpless and very sad."

Mary suggested a Nurtured Heart Approach parenting class that would be taught by herself and Stephanie Rule. Anna and Todd agreed and began to read the book required by the course (they use the *Transforming the Difficult Child Workbook* written by Lisa Bravo, Joann Bowdidge and myself). "The Nurtured Heart philosophy felt strange to us," Anna told me. "It forced us to pass through the negatives and get to a place of love and encouragement, especially in the line of fire. But we thought 'what the heck,' it can't hurt and we don't have any other options. It's either this or military school."

The couple dug in their heels and began the journey hand in hand. Sean was initially angered by the positive acknowledgements that make up the core of this approach. His reaction was: "What are you doing? Why are you acting like this? Something is different and I don't like it. STOP IT NOW!" Things got worse. Sean would mimic and laugh at his parents, but they stuck with it—often calling on their mentor, Celeste Elsey, when they weren't sure how to proceed. According to Anna, "Celeste taught us how to just turn our backs on him and reset, both for his sake and ours. There were calls to her day and night, asking what to say, how to handle a situation, how to win this war." (You will learn, as you read on, what a 'reset' is and why it is so critical not to accidentally feed the negative choices of a child who is being difficult.)

In the space of a very stressful two weeks, Anna and Todd mastered the art of giving radical recognitions to their son at every opportunity when he wasn't being abusive and hostile. In response, Sean built stronger walls. When Sean asked them what had changed and why they were acting like this, they answered, "We were wrong to focus on the bad and miss out on all of the wonderful things you've done. We've been missing out on your greatness and we don't want to miss any more!" They told him that this was going to be their way with him and his siblings from then on, so he might as well get used to it. He continued to taunt and make fun of them. And they continued to play "hardball" with the approach.

"Then one day, a few weeks in, we noticed a softening in Sean," Anna told me. "At first it was small, but gradually, over the course of a week, the old Sean came back. The venomous side of him was losing its battle and love was winning." They continued with lots of self-control, lots of resetting, lots of loss of control and mistakes, and lots of phone calls to Celeste, but they were starting to see the dawn.

These parents felt their son had returned to them by the end of May 2009. Since then, Sean has been able to live as his true self: a bright, generous, kind and sensitive young man who gets good grades. He now enjoys school for the first time in his life, has self-confidence and is proud of himself. The only thing that caused these changes was their use of the Nurtured Heart Approach. Eventually, Anna and Todd found they could relax their application of the approach on some days and apply it less intensely when they did use it. "We still battle the challenges Sean is faced with, and it is still hard," Anna shared, "but thankfully, we have a tool that helps us get through those challenges in a nurturing way."

So you won't see much talk about diagnoses of any kind in this book; they are irrelevant in this context. The approach is applied in a similar manner with every child, diagnosable or not. Back in the early days when I was just starting out with my 'cure' for ADHD, I had enough faith in what was happening that I kept finding ways to amp it up to reach ever more difficult and troubled children. Now, I see clearly how indebted I am to those children, because it was they who got this approach to *cook*. Eventually it became a mode of treatment that could be ramped up when called for to have profound impact on even the toughest children. Kids were being pulled back from the brink.

It wasn't long before it became evident that the Nurtured Heart Approach, while created initially for difficult children, has merit for every child. Every child needs abundant inner strength to handle the stresses of modern life. A child who needs a stronger intervention gets a more "notched-up" version than a less difficult child, but the bones of the approach are the same no matter what the child's perceived behavior issues or symptoms. (Throughout this book, you'll see boxed sections entitled "Notch it Up" as well as "Notching it Up" sections between the chapters, both of which give techniques about how to more intensely apply the approach when necessary.)

In the early days of turning my 'silly notions' into an effective therapeutic approach for challenging children, other therapists became curious about what I was doing. I resisted pressure to share my methods. For one thing, I feared that the approach was too idiosyncratic to be accepted in the therapeutic community. I couldn't see a way to explain coherently to other professionals what I was doing. And on top of all that, I hated public speaking.

Eventually, though, an agency persuaded me to give an in-service for its therapists. I felt painfully awkward and afterward promised myself I'd never do it again.

About a month later, while at the grocery store, I happened to see someone who'd attended my in-service. This therapist was head of the agency's family preservation unit and supervised 10 counselors in trying to help an unending array of challenging children in an unending array of difficult situations. When he told me that his team was using my approach almost exclusively—with great results—my life flashed before my eyes. I knew without question that my new job was to spread the word.

At the Center for the Difficult Child, which opened in 1994, I trained therapists in this approach, which by then was called the Nurtured Heart Approach. They became incredibly effective. This was even true of interns who had not yet graduated from their degree programs. Much to the dismay of more established agencies, we quickly became the sought-after internship in the area.

Fast-forward to today, about a decade and a half later. I have become much more comfortable giving presentations, and I've authored and co-authored several books based on the application and continual 'cooking' or refining of the approach. The original book, *Transforming the Difficult Child*, is now used in nearly every part of the world.

Notch it Up: *Greatness Is a Given*

You might have heard someone say to you, or you might have told someone else, that you or they have *great qualities.* Certainly, this is true; every person can be celebrated for such qualities. We all have them. But I want to encourage you to consider this: the positive traits, behaviors and choices you are demonstrating and making in this very moment aren't things you put on, like your clothes, or ideas you come up with, like the idea of going to catch a 9:30 movie. They are *expressions of the greatness you already possess.* That greatness is your birthright—and it is the birthright of every human being.

This is the beginning of notching up the approach: seeing the truth of your own inherent greatness and that of everyone around you. Naming and celebrating that greatness is a matter of connecting with what shines most brightly to you in any given moment.

At my Advanced Trainings, I and a small handful of fellow leaders have guided nearly one thousand educators, treatment professionals and parents through a week-long process, at the end of which they become Certified Nurtured Heart Approach Advanced Trainers. This gives them all they need to apply the approach with greater depth and intensity in their schools, offices and homes and to conduct their own trainings. The approach continues to spread into homes, classrooms, treatment facilities, programs and therapy offices.

Now, you stand poised at the brink of learning how you can apply this same approach in your work as an educator or educational administrator. I want to take a moment to acknowledge the greatness of this step you're taking.

In seeking out new and better ways to support your students, you are demonstrating assertiveness, bravery, open-mindedness and a desire to keep growing yourself in ways that will promote the greatness of each student you encounter. You are embodying discipline (it's a lot to ask of a busy professional, these days, to read a book all the way through), determined application and focus. In seeking new wisdom, you are showing a willingness to learn something new and a determination to apply it in spite of previous attempts that could have led you to give up. You are willing to discern what may not be working and are willing to let that motivate you to seek further knowledge, even though that might contradict previous studies. You are choosing a positive way to orchestrate your classroom, rather than choosing punishment, yelling, lecturing, nagging, pawning off troublesome children to administrators or telling parents that their child should be on Ritalin. These are all qualities of your greatness.

We've all met educators who are not willing to take the time or trouble to look at something new, so the truth is that in seeking to learn more, you are making a decision that contains and conveys good judgment, wisdom, compassion and caring. I consider these, too, to be qualities of greatness.

Take a few seconds, right now, to cloak yourself in this incontrovertible evidence of your successful choice. Sit back and let yourself feel energized by it.

Chapter 2
Energy Rules

IN MY PRESENTATIONS FOR EDUCATORS, I usually ask for a show of hands from those who feel that their training adequately prepared them to deal with discipline issues. Sometimes I see a hand or two, but most often not a single hand goes up.

These groups of educators also affirm that each year brings more difficult children to their classrooms than the year before and that the level of intensity of these children is on the rise. The incredible 50 percent attrition rate among educators during their first three years of teaching obviously stems in large part from the difficulty of coping with children who act out day after day despite teachers' best efforts to impose discipline.

It's the rare teacher who enters his or her first classroom feeling as though he or she knows how to control kids who are exquisitely skilled at upending the whole classroom whenever they feel like it. For that matter, the average parent ends up feeling ill-equipped at handling disciplinary problems. This lack of facility can't be blamed on any shortage of expert advice on these topics: at this writing, the popular web-based bookstore Amazon.com has nearly 120,000 titles on the topic of parenting, more than 25,000 on child discipline and 20,000-plus on behavior modification.

These experts are offering their very best advice. Nobody's trying to create an unsuccessful kid. It's just that the methods proffered in almost every one of these books aren't working for a growing proportion of children. They may have worked in the past and may still work for some, but today a growing number of challenging children seem to require more.

The prevailing opinion is that if a child cannot be managed through conventional means, medications are the next logical step. In 1985, about half a million U.S. children were taking stimulant drugs for ADHD; today, that number is up to about six million. Between 1995 and 1999, antidepressant use increased 580 percent in the six-and-under population and 151 percent in children aged seven to 12.[1] In 1993, just over 200,000 children were diagnosed with bipolar disorder and placed on antipsychotic drugs; in 2002, that number soared to 1,224,000.[2] This stratospheric rise in psychiatric diagnoses and medicating of children provides further evidence that a new direction is required.

---

1. Citizens' Commission on Human Rights, www.CCHR.org
2. Olfson M, et al, "National trends in the outpatient treatment of children and adolescents with antipsychotic drugs," *Archives of General Psychology* 2006 Jun; 63(6):679-85.

The approach you will learn in this book is just that: an effective alternative. It is about giving children an unshakable sense of self-worth with which they can navigate the complex territory of modern life. They learn to use their intensity to propel success rather than to break rules and create chaos.

Upside-Down Energy

Imagine yourself, for a moment, in a classroom. Your students are working diligently on a project in their groups. Everyone's cooperating. Everyone's staying on task. What do you do? Most likely, you tiptoe over to your desk to get some pressing tasks accomplished before the next disruption. You might even sit back quietly and enjoy the sight of your beloved students getting so much out of their educational experience.

Then, a couple of students start to argue and their voices rise, disrupting the others in the room. Now what happens? On a good day, you start with a gentle reminder to get focused on their work again. When this doesn't work, still on that proverbial good day, you might go to the students, gently insert yourself into the fracas, and try to help the kids work out their differences. You might give a 'sermon' about the importance of respecting the others' need for quiet in order to get their work done or about cooperation within their group. And on that good day, you might well give one or two or more warnings before exacting any consequence or escalating your response to the problem.

On a bad day, you might not give a single warning, jumping right to some form of reprimand, heated reaction or worse. Either way, you have demonstrated the same fundamental message to the students: when they are behaving themselves and following the rules, they get little or no response from you; but when they threaten to break a rule or cross the line into actually breaking a rule, suddenly they have intense, highly present interest, connection and relationship with you.

Adults tend to get really tuned-in when things are going wrong. We shift into high gear to attack problems, dismantle and analyze them, and search for fixes and solutions. The Nurtured Heart Approach is not designed to solve problems or to address specific misbehaviors or even to address specific misbehaving children. At the foundation of this approach is a *refusal to focus on problems.* We don't put any energy into figuring out what the problems are or why they exist. We don't pour energy toward developing solutions or techniques for solving those problems. Along these same lines, we also do not single out the children who create problems. The approach is applied to every child in the classroom.

We aren't pretending problems don't exist. But we don't want to pour gas on the fire of what the child already perceives: that problems are the most efficient route to juicy connectivity and relationship. Instead, we bring our main focus to what's going right: on recognizing, in honest and satisfying detail, the child's successes, good choices, following of rules and other positive behaviors.

The perception that this approach seeks to change in the child is that he can only exact relationship when acting out. It is not a method for behavior modification but rather a way to excite the spirits and souls of children that also happens to modify the behavior of those who are disruptive. *We have resoundingly found that when we inspire the greatness of children, they act out greatness.*

We inspire children to express this innate greatness by **removing all energy from responses to students' negative choices (aside from providing an unenergized consequence when a rule is broken); and by energizing the many positive choices students make *in the moments those choices are being made.***

This approach teaches how to see success where it might have gone unnoticed before, and how to *create* success where it might not otherwise appear to exist. You'll learn how to acknowledge that success to students in convincing detail; how to treat each moment as a new opportunity for success; how to make rules crystal clear; and how to create an unceremonious and effective consequence as soon as those rules are broken.

The truth is that relationship with you, the educator, is the most ardently sought incentivizing energy in any classroom. The children in your charge are often looking for connection with and feedback from you. They are not just looking for attention; they're looking for *energized relationship,* which is a more textured kind of connection. Even if you can't quite wrap your mind around this, trust me: it's the energetic truth. Your faith in the fact that *YOUR energy and relationship are the biggest "gift" in the room* will give you a big leg up as you begin to work with this approach.

Even if you seem to be the very last thing on their minds, the fact is that they are looking to you, in every moment, for 'juice'—for your focus and connectivity. If you are energetically responsive to them when they are making poor choices and are relatively distracted or low-key when they are being 'good,' you inadvertently demonstrate to them that under-functioning or bad behavior is required to create satisfying relationship with you. In every moment, they drink in impressions about the energetic truth of how the world and the people in it really operate, and most children conclude very early in life that this truth boils down to something like this: *misbehavior is the quickest, most reliable way to meet my need for intimate connection with others—particularly the adult in the room.*

Ultimately, what we energize is what we show love for. And so, with traditional disciplinary methods that inadvertently create intense relationship around misbehavior, you wind up accidentally showing your students that you love and care about them more when they misbehave or threaten to misbehave. We are typically so much more *there* when things are going wrong.

How We Accidentally 'Energize' Children for Breaking the Rules

On a day when I was scheduled to give a school in-service, I arrived while the school day was still in session and was shown to the library, where a class was in progress. As I set up my equipment in an adjoining part of the large space, a librarian/teacher sat at her desk doing her own work. At this point the students were going about their business, working mostly independently; at times they worked cooperatively and with full focus. As everything went smoothly, there was no interaction at all with the teacher. Then one boy began to create a minor disruption, which drew the teacher out of her seat as though she had a hook in her mouth.

This teacher was clearly a *kind and loving* person who seemed compelled to get to this child as quickly as possible. In a *kind and loving* manner, she took the boy aside, gently put her arm around his shoulders and launched a conversation. I could hear her *kindly and lovingly* telling him not to be disruptive, to be quiet and respectful to his classmates, and to stay focused and get his project completed. And, finally, in a *kind and loving way*, she released him back to his table, with obvious faith in the impact of her words.

This child had stumbled upon a 'button' that created an experience of loving attention. Certainly, he knew that he had broken a rule. He knew that he was being told to behave differently. But beneath the content of her communication was a delicious reward of connection, relationship and energy. Whether you call it a chat, a reprimand, a lecture, a life lesson, a pep talk, a diatribe, a sermonette, an instruction, or an admonition, the energetic meta-message was upside-down from the one intended. This boy soon created a new disruption and several other children soon followed suit.

The inadvertent energetic message of this teacher's response to this student was: *When you do the right thing in my room, you are relatively invisible; when you act out in disruptive ways, you are the recipient of…kind and loving relationship.* **No educator would send this message on purpose, but it happens like this in schools around the world every second of every day.**

Although she was indeed kind and loving, this teacher was energizing negativity. Her heart-felt intention was beautiful and her aim was to support and teach—but her timing was upside-down. I don't want her to stop being *kind and loving;* I just want her to turn that timing right-side-up. The Nurtured Heart Approach is a way of giving that kindness and love at the right time, in an energetically congruent way: when children are making choices to *not* break rules.

If I'm a teacher and have a thing for respectfulness, I focus on other things when my students are being respectful. When a child is disrespectful, however, I snap to attention. I become much more present and verbally adamant that this is not okay. My students interpret this as a clear message that I am more available for caring connection when disrespect is happening.

A verbal (or even nonverbal) warning or a threatened consequence might be enough to stop the average child from causing problems just to get a hit of adult connection. But for the child who is more intense and needy, it's not a real deterrent. They need the juice more than they fear the consequences. With this approach, educators refuse to give that juice when things go wrong. Instead of giving energy to negativity, *they tenaciously seek out opportunities to give it when things are going right.*

Let's use the imaginary classroom as an example. Let's say that in those moments when your class is quiet and everyone's working hard, you make a few specific 'energizing' statements:

"Wow, I can see that Jenny is really focused on figuring out the first step of the directions. Way to apply yourself, Jenny! And Shawn has taken responsibility for writing down the input of all his group members during the brainstorm. Tonia is offering to help Frank assemble the group's materials; that's great collaboration." And so on.

If Tonia and Frank start to become irritated with one another, you quickly scan the situation to see what's going right—*before anyone actually breaks a rule.* You might say, loud enough to be overheard by the entire room: "Tonia, I can see you're getting frustrated with the way Frank wants to organize the materials. I want to commend you for handling your strong feelings so well. And Frank, thank you for not raising your voice. I can see you're finding a solution, just the two of you." You also make a point of verbally recognizing a couple of other children who are working peacefully and quietly, following the rules and getting the project done: "I see Hannah is focused on her work, despite the distraction, and is cutting strips of red and purple paper. I also see Jonas taking out the glue to start assembling the project he's doing with Hannah."

Can you see how this shows children that it's juicy and rewarding to do the right thing? How the students are being energized for just doing what they're supposed to do? In stark contrast to energizing the good that is happening, this approach also strives to make rule-breaking boring and uninteresting.

Ever have students push your negative buttons so astutely that you wonder why they are out to 'get you?' This approach is about getting students to push the *positive* buttons because they create the fireworks once reserved for negative behaviors. When they push the negative buttons, it's as though the machine's batteries have just died. They get no energy, no sparks, no histrionics. In its place, they experience only an un-energized reset from the action—

which then transitions seamlessly back into the energy of all that's right.

The Nurtured Heart Approach seeks to build children's inner wealth through *concrete experiences of being successful—irrefutable evidence of living and being greatness—as reflected back to them by caring adults.* In my trainings, I use a clip from "The Horse Whisperer"—a heartbreaking but ultimately joyous film—to explain to participants how this works.

"It's Not a Question of Whether You Can or Can't...You Are."

In this film, Grace, a girl of about 13, is hit by a truck while horseback riding with her best friend. The friend and the friend's horse are killed, and one of Grace's legs has to be amputated to save her life. Grace's horse is badly injured and traumatized. In an effort to bring the girl out of a deep depression, her mother brings Grace and her horse to Tom, a 'horse whisperer' who has a legendary way with these animals. She hopes he will help the horse recover and that this will help Grace re-enter her life as well.

Tom calls Grace out of the stable one day and offers to teach her how to drive his pickup truck. She protests that she's too young, she can't because of her leg and so on. But Tom calmly eggs her on until she's in the driver's seat of the truck with the motor running.

"Go ahead and give it some gas," he tells her. She does, and the truck lurches forward. Discouraged, she looks over at him. "Now you know you can," he tells her. "Now you just gotta figure out how much." She tries again. Soon the truck is chugging along at a reasonable pace. "Now just keep driving until you run out of road," Tom tells her, adding "I think I'll just close my eyes for a little while." He pushes the brim of his Stetson down over his eyes and scooches down, folding his arms across his belly. "But...I don't think I can," Grace feebly protests. "It's not a question of whether you can or you can't. You *are*," Tom replies.

Tom didn't brightly bark "good job!" and "way to go!" and "you're terrific!" Did he give her a trophy just for getting in the car? Absolutely not. He downloaded an experience of success by fundamentally *tripping* her into doing something she didn't think she could do and then handing her all of the credit in the moment in which she was being successful. He didn't argue with her or tell her how disappointed he was when she initially resisted his invitation to learn to drive the truck. He didn't lecture or reprimand her when she initially over-accelerated. Instead, he calmly but relentlessly kept leading her toward a true experience of success and then irrefutably staked claim to that moment.

These moments are the stuff from which inner wealth is built. We don't always need to trick the child into success. Everyday moments where nothing dramatic seems to be happening are fair game, too. But the more difficult the child, the more likely that you'll have to mount some clever maneuvers like

27

the one Tom did with Grace. This is *not* about 'catching the child being good,' but about *creating*, with intention, powerful experiences of success for the child.

Improvement vs. Transformation

Inner wealth is the foundation upon which students can rely to make sound choices as they chart their courses in life. This approach therapeutically creates that inner wealth. It is *not* about 'improvement'—the Holy Grail often held up by proponents of Ritalin and other medications used to control behaviors that spring from a difficult child's intensity. Even if the medications give the illusion of improvement, the problems are still there before the meds kick in and when they wear off. They haven't gone away.

With improvement, the adult is still essentially relating to problems. In contrast, this approach fosters a *transformation* that enables a child to channel his intensity toward bringing out the greatness that is his birthright. Transformation happens when adults learn powerful ways of making any moment an opportunity to create experiences of success and greatness for students. We have much more opportunity to do this than you might think.

Notch it Up: *The Good, the Bad and the Great*

This transformation entails a shift from traditional "good vs. bad" thinking where children come to believe that they need to be *good;* and that if they aren't being good, they're possibly being *bad.* Adults strive to teach goodness by teaching children how to be good people and by modeling good behavior. But this good/bad dichotomy gets muddied because the world is so highly energized around what's bad. 'Bad' behavior is what our eyes come to see and what we end up railing against. It can consume a fair amount of our energy and can become a breeding ground of fear and worry. A constant threat looms: we might slip into the gravitational pull of the opposite of good.

This approach transcends this dichotomy by notching goodness up into greatness. Greatness isn't weighed down by 'not-greatness'; it doesn't have a diametric opposite. As the 13th century Sufi poet Rumi wrote: "Out beyond ideas of rightdoing and wrongdoing, there is a field. I'll meet you there." That field is greatness.

Seeing things this way creates more impetus to use whatever's not right as energy to grow further into greatness—a topic we'll cover in detail in later chapters.

Toys 'R' Us

Imagine presenting a child with a brand-new toy: an electronic gadget with lights, buttons, levers and other alluring features. It makes sounds, vibrates and lights up in many colors.

The typical child doesn't ask for the instruction manual; she just starts to play. She pokes it, prods it, shakes it, tries all of the buttons and levers, turns it this way and that. Features that offer the most captivating energy are the ones typical children will find worth revisiting. If a button gets pushed or a lever gets thrown without any compelling result, she might try it again once or twice to see if it remains the same, or she might go back to it a few times by accident. Eventually she'll decide that this feature is disconnected or boring and will quit expending any effort there—especially if other functions of the toy provide a connected, enthralling experience.

Children form impressions of the world and their effect upon it through exactly this kind of direct experience. Starting at birth, children form these impressions through doing, manipulating, participating and observing. Little by little, they develop their take on how the world works and on their impact on the world. Once they're big enough, children do this with toys; but from the beginnings of their lives, they do this with people—particularly with important adults. From birth, children observe and experiment interactively with these adults. They drink in impressions based on the truth of what they experience.

One way of construing this is that adults are, for all intents and purposes, *children's favorite toys*. We are the most interesting, interactive, multi-featured elements in children's lives—children's ultimate entertainment centers.

When the acting-out begins, adults get really entertaining. We are more present, engaged, energized, alive, animated and connected. We're more willing to devote time and energy, qualitatively and quantitatively. Children quickly realize that, in response to their acting-out, they get greater closeness— longer conversations, more vivid animation or heightened emotion. Essentially, more intimacy flows in response to problems. Children see that the top-shelf version of deep connection can reliably be achieved by way of poor choices. On the other hand, when things are going right, adults are relatively boring. Just as with real toys, they write off the boring features and habitually go with those they perceive to yield more excitement and energy.

We typically respond to a child's poor choices with world-class lectures, pleading, reasoning, cajoling, arguing, nagging or reprimands. And then we somehow believe the child will find these measures irresistibly compelling enough to inspire them to change their ways. We think our rational words of reason and wisdom will win the day because they will make so much sense to the child. However: children experience the truth of what gets us going. They detect the river of energy beneath our words; the message they get is that we are a lot more available and exciting when things are going wrong.

How much energy do *you* radiate when your students do as you say? Is it Tigger energy (*bouncy! bouncy! bouncy!*) or Eeyore energy (*thaaank yoooou…*)? What flows when students misbehave? Most often, it's big energy, big emotion, big involvement.

In the realm of what children relish in toys, adults are pretty darned incredible. Compared with anything made in a toy factory, they have an almost limitless array of buttons, levers, switches and more variations in response, volume, mood and action. By the time a child starts school, she has learned quite well which actions, moods, modes, refusals and stories get the responses that best feed her needs—at which point she habitually seeks similar reactivity from her teachers. To get this compelling response, the child becomes more and more willing to risk reprimand or punishment. He or she gets energized through these stronger connections via negativity.

For every child, and for the difficult child in particular, *energy rules.* Show me a kid who's a little more alive or intense, and who is predominantly exposed to normal, traditional and conventional forms of parenting and teaching, and I'll show you a kid who is more likely to form the impression that these 'toys'—the adults in their lives—are much more interesting when things go wrong.

When you think of a child "pushing your buttons," you most likely think of that child figuring out what makes you mad. Indeed, these are usually the buttons that children push—because they yield the quickest and most reliably fascinating responses. Adults tend to be most animated and available under problematic circumstances. Such circumstances generally yield instantaneous and deep connection and relationship. The energy they receive in response to negative behaviors may not be in the form of angry outbursts; it may be more subtle, as in the case of a kind and loving admonishment or heartfelt discussion. It's still much more profound than when things are going along just fine, during which time most responses are muted.

If this Toys 'R' Us story is making sense to you, start to consider a radical shift: choose to *no longer give your energy to negativity*—in any of its many manifestations.

Content vs. Connection

My co-author Melissa recently met a charming family of four while waiting to board a flight at the airport. The parents were positive and patient with their rambunctious children. While they all waited in line to board, the four-year-old girl repeatedly grabbed and hugged her two-year-old brother, which made him squeal and push her away. The mother said affectionately, "Stop that, now.

He doesn't like it, and every time you do that, he's going to do the same thing!"

A moment of peace ensued. The parents were quiet, looking straight ahead, no doubt steeling themselves for a three-hour flight with two kids under the age of five. The girl's eyes went back toward her brother, and she began to sidle in his direction. The look on her face was something between trepidation (about getting scolded again) and determination (to go for 'more'—unwittingly drawn to see how much intimacy she might get this time around).

Melissa offered a diversion by asking the girl her name and giving her a verbal appreciation: "I see you're tempted to grab your brother, but you're making a choice to hold off." Immediately, the girl focused on Melissa. For the moment, she didn't need to push limits in an effort to get the more highly energized albeit negative relationship with mom and dad.

We all have needs for closeness and connection. Whether you call it relationship or intimacy, you're talking about the quality and magnitude of the energy we project and our own perception of energy coming our way from others. It is conveyed by how 'present' and alive we are in the presence of others. Our energy is also conveyed by the *texture* of our presence and aliveness: the level of emotion, excitement and love conveyed in our actions.

Through this lens, start watching the children around you in their interactions with adults. If you have your own children, watch them carefully without yet changing what you've been doing to discipline them. Do you ever see that same look (the one just described on the face of the little girl in the airport) on their faces when they're preparing to do the opposite of what they've been told? Notice how, when they break the rule and get a consequence or an energized response, they don't seem too bothered. They aren't bothered by some measly little consequence (or even a great big consequence) because *they have obtained YOU, and they know it!* They controlled the situation in a way that handed them *THE* prize in the room, just as they expected it would. Although it might feel, at times, like the child is out to ruin your day, what he's after is that feeling of connection.

When Tommy is being lectured by his parent, he hears words: "Tommy, now you *know* your mom does not like it when you roll your eyes at her. It's disrespectful, it's rude, and I know you know better, Tommy. I need you to never roll your eyes at your mother again. Is that clear?"

What Tommy gets, though, is an energetic message that illuminates and verifies the fact that the parent radiates a lot more energy in the aftermath of bad behavior than during good behavior. In response to this lecture, Tommy does not experience an epiphany that inspires him to say, "I have realized my error! I can't believe I was so disrespectful and rude to the woman who gave me life. I'll never disrespect Mom by rolling my eyes at her—never again—my solemn promise." More likely, Tommy sits there wearing the mask that says he's listening when he's completely tuned out. Or, if he's a difficult child like I was, he might do some version of what I used to do when my father would lecture me: I'd cross my arms over my chest and raise a middle finger at him beneath each armpit. (One day he finally caught me. That was not a good day for obvious reasons, but it did yield intense relationship with my dad—which was hard to come by when I was not making poor choices.)

In communications with children, adults tend to hold fast to the notion that we are being interpreted literally. But there is an energetic currency that underlies the rational, reasonable, logical and straightforward messages we attempt to convey. Our words are the lapping surface of the water, but our energy is the massive power of the current beneath. The energy beneath our words is more powerful than their meaning, especially for children.

Just as children seek an energized response while investigating that new toy, they seek out that river of energy beneath our words. There's the *content* of communications, but beneath that is the far more powerful *connection*—the degree or magnitude of perceived relationship that is created during that communication. And that connection—the relationship—is primary for children.

Think about your computer connection. Do you want to go back to dial-up? Of course not—dial-up is sluggish and boring compared to newer forms of high-speed connectivity. Once children know intuitively where connection is faster and more abundant, they go unhesitatingly toward it, regardless of the content of our words. Major shifts in the way we interact with them are required to demonstrate that doing the right things can bring the same lightning-fast connectivity they now associate with acting out. Let's go for the broadband of greatness!

If I held up a $5 and a $50 bill, which would you pick? How long would it take you to figure out which one carries a greater 'charge?' You would know immediately which has greater value—which will get you *more*. And children learn early on that, while they might get a few watered-down words of praise when they follow the rules, the fastest and most reliable way to get to those flashing lights, interesting sounds and dynamic movements—the lightning rods of life-force—from the adult in the room is by acting out and breaking rules.

Here's another story to illustrate the divide between content and connection, this one from early childhood educator Pat Bethke:

We finish our school day with snacks and the expectation that these independent three-year-olds will clean up their table areas, put on their coats, hats, and mittens, grab their school bags, and return to their seats for dismissal. Most have no problem with this scenario…but then there's Sam.

Before I began to use the Nurtured Heart Approach, the end of the day sounded something like this: "Sam, are you done with your snack? What do you need to do next? Sam, would you please throw your cup away? Sam, what should you be doing now? Sam, we are not reading books. Sam, your coat is still hanging up. Sam, look where everyone is right now—I think the moms and dads are waiting to pick you up!" And finally, I would take Sam gently by the hand, walk him over to his coat, and quickly, lovingly proceed to dress him. All the other children were waiting in their spots...waiting for Sam to finish his routine so that they could sing the good-bye song and go home.

I realized something: I was teaching Sam that he was incapable of getting himself ready to go home. I was giving him the impression that he was not independent like his classmates. I was accidentally nurturing his defiance!

Sam was reaching the incontrovertible conclusion that he got more out of life by refusing to get ready to go home at the end of the day. This kind and loving teacher would readily give him one-on-one time in exchange for his refusal to comply with even the simplest request. Do you see what the other students might be learning from Sam's example?

Here's how Pat's story about Sam ended happily:

One year later, in the same classroom but with the Nurtured Heart Approach in place, this is how the scenario plays out:

"Sam, you are almost done with your snack! Megan is throwing her trash away. Sam is getting up and heading to the garbage. Olivia is getting her coat! And there goes Sam, heading for his coat. Charlie, you're working hard at getting your fingers in your gloves, what great patience. Sam's got his coat on and is working on his mittens. Sam, you're so independent! I see lots of friends waiting at their table spots. You're showing me how responsible you are! And there's Sam, slipping right into his spot! What collaborative energy in this room!" I give a little cheer. Successful, independent and responsible Sam is smiling!

Some children seem to rise to these occasions of exacting connection for negativity far faster and with much greater energy than others. The button-pushing of the girl in the airport was subtle; other children seem totally devoted to this endeavor. Many intense children have jammed the lion's share of their power and intelligence into a convoluted pattern of behavior that is all about taking their quest for maximum adult energy to any extreme necessary. This is a terrible waste of their brilliance.

Does the child who chooses to break a rule know what the rules are? Almost always, yes. Is she capable of controlling herself? Yes, but not as long as she believes that her needs are best met through negativity. She knows full well that breaking the rules is the purest, surest way to get energized relationship in a flash. Can this be shifted in a way that cultivates greatness? Absolutely yes!

The Moving Target

The energy of a curriculum-based lesson most often conveys little or no direct relationship in a classroom setting. Seemingly positive statements like "good job" and "thanks" are energetically low-key conveyances of connection. When things are going well and curriculum is flowing, teachers tend to unintentionally pare down the energy they offer to their students. However, when rules are broken—even when there is a *threat* of a rule being broken—that's when the real energetic exchange lifts off.

Depending on the teacher and on what sort of day he or she is having, there might be anything from warnings to gentle attempts at redirection to a volcanic eruption of adult emotional energy. Multiple repetitions of lukewarm versions of "thanks" and "good job" in return for staying within the bounds of the rules pale in comparison to the energy radiated in relation to adversity.

Warnings are most often counterproductive, as we'll explain in detail later. They are gas on the very fire you want to put out, and they are neon signs advertising that the student can count on you for more vivid and energized response if he *does* go ahead with whatever behavior you're warning him against.

It's as though his toy had a few buttons that gave different and special responses every time they were pushed. Sometimes, the response is high definition; at others, it's just ho-hum. It's unsettling but compelling to keep going back there to see what will happen the next time they're pushed.

Oops, You Broke a Rule—Here's a Hundred Bucks

According to this logic, an energized response from an adult to a rule being broken (admonition, warning, lecture or energized consequence) is, unfortunately, an incentive. This is very confusing for the child. No one would ever dream of giving a child $100 for breaking a rule, but energetically, much of the time we inadvertently give that and more in response to problems, issues and rule-breaking.

On subtle levels, even pep talks and attempts to encourage end up energizing the child when he's *not* succeeding. Beneath "Come on, Sarah, you can do it!" is a very different energetic truth: "Apparently, Sarah, at the moment, you're *not* doing it, and I am captivated enough by this to give you an enlivened response."

We typically offer lectures, diatribes and instruction about desirable values when the desired behaviors or values are not present. When a child is disrespectful, he gets a big lecture about being respectful. Energetically, this

34

communicates to the child: "You are disrespectful, and when you are, *I'm right here for you.*"

Fifty years ago, no matter what the student's need for adult energy, the fear of a severe, possibly corporal consequence for poor behavior served to suppress children's energy-seeking efforts. Many would argue that fear-based interventions are of value due to the simple fact that they appear to work. Sure, they might do the job of keeping kids in line, but they do so at a steep price: affecting children's potential for realizing their full greatness.

As a society we've moved away from punitive, fear-based disciplinary approaches in hopes of raising children who are creative, courageous, intelligent and able to think outside the box. In this, we've partially succeeded. Fear has largely been removed as a deterrent, and that's a good thing, but no truly effective alternative has taken its place.

Modern disciplinary methods are effective with less intense, less difficult children, but they so often backfire with more intense children. In many schools, eight percent of students seem to take 80 percent of the resources. We've got a great many spirited, intense, energy-seeking kids on our hands, and they aren't afraid of us. They're being lost by the truckload. New methods are needed to transmute this energy away from rule-breaking, boundary-pushing and oppositional behavior and into expressions of greatness.

The Energy-Challenged Child

If this notion that you are one of a difficult child's "favorite toys" makes sense to you, then you can see how he wants to play it for the biggest possible exchange of energy. He prefers to get that energy from the most important person in the room, and in your classroom, that's you. **You are the gift to be sought. You are the most important source of available connection and life force in his immediate future.** For now, when he's in your classroom, you are the only game in town.

To some extent, every child is wired to try to connect energetically with adults. Some children need more energy association than others. In the classroom, these children display behaviors including hyperactivity, impulsivity, defiance, obtuseness, frequent verbal outbursts or any other form of aggression, anxiety, depressive withdrawal, shyness, extreme sensitivity, a habit of not keeping one's hands to one's self, distractibility, lack of participation, lack of academic engagement, or other more nuanced poor choices.

Some children need so much intense energy that they do not hesitate to behave abominably in order to get that need met. Their need for perceived energetic payoff can easily exceed their fear of punishment or other consequences. Some children are going to go for the biggest experience of energy they can get from their favorite toy, even if that toy is going to blow up or break as a result.

A child's high need for energy can be tamped down with medications. This has become the method of choice for intense and difficult children. A child who learns to control his intensity without medications—who learns to turn his intensity *toward greatness*—is more likely to flourish than a child whose intensity is moderated by substances. Although a medicated child might seem improved, this kind of improvement harbors suffering under its surface. His problems haven't gone away, and he's no more able to handle them once the meds are stopped. These medications do not cure and they do not heal. They tamp down the child's life force and send a message to the child that he can't handle it, and neither can we.

An Alternative to Drugging Difficult Children

During the writing of my book *100 Reasons to Avoid Ritalin Like the Plague*, I chose to take this medication for 10 days under the close watch of my physician. (It was no problem for me to fit into the diagnostic criteria for ADHD, so it was all perfectly legal.) The dose I took was low, but I definitely felt it, and whenever something went well, I wondered: *is it me or the drug?* When something went badly, was it me or the drug? Rote tasks came easily (I got a lot of housework done), but I didn't trust myself to do anything really important while I was taking Ritalin. I didn't feel like myself or believe in myself and I couldn't put my finger on my impact on the world. I experienced a progressively deepening estrangement with success. I wasn't really living. I couldn't put my finger on that deep place from which my spark of inspiration arises. I was hanging on for dear life.

No one wants difficult, intense kids to be put on more and more meds and end up with exquisite careers as mental health patients. I believe that every parent and every educator would rather see children thrive without depending on medications.[3] Still, there's no question that schools are encountering more and more students who are acting out at unprecedented levels. Sometimes medications seem like the only realistic way to handle this in the school setting.

There is an alternative: for educators to learn ways to channel students' intensity into greatness in ways that align with the rules and regulations of society without having to resort to powerful psychotropic medications. This is possible for virtually every child, even the ones who seem intractably difficult and impossible to reach. In classrooms and schools that implement the

---

3. For parents or teachers who are interested in learning about natural ways to remedy ADHD symptoms, I recommend the book by Sanford Newmark, MD: *ADHD Without Drugs: A Guide to the Natural Care of Children with ADHD by one of America's Leading Integrative Physicians* (Nurtured Heart Publications, 2010). Dr. Newmark, a close colleague of Dr. Andrew Weil, understands the Nurtured Heart Approach well and recommends it as an integral part of his non-drug ADHD protocol.

approach taught in this book, referrals for psychiatric testing and the use of medications like Ritalin almost always fall to nearly zero.

Think of a child you know who seems to be out of control, or even *out to get you*—who will go to the proverbial mat in his efforts to make you lose your cool. Now, think of that child's quest to get your goat in terms of his *thirst for energy, connection and relationship*. He isn't a bad child; he's an energy-challenged child.

My experience is that even with the most challenging child, all is never lost and positive relationship can always win in the long run. Every child is retrievable when we learn to work with the energy at the foundation of each interaction. Medications might be helpful in a fraction of cases, but in most, they become unnecessary once a child is shown the way to his own intrinsic greatness. This is my interpretation of "no child left behind."

The worst child in your class is a product of real-life experiences that have convinced him that acting out is the only way for him to reliably obtain the level of connection he craves. He does not yet trust that connection is available sufficiently or consistently through any positive means. This is a portrait of the *energy-challenged child*.

The length of time for which this pattern has been established or how it was established is inconsequential. Some children innately have more intensity than they can handle. Some children are, from birth, prone to overwhelm in response to all that is stirring within them. Others become more intense at some point in their lives in response to their life circumstances (such as exposure to neglect or abuse or other arenas of stress, worry, fear or doubt). And even the 'best' child has her moments of over-the-top intensity.

Whether it's purely physical intensity, emotional intensity or any other form of overbearing life force, or whether it's a response to circumstances, *intensity that currently runs amok via acting-out can be shifted*. It can become magical—a gift. This shift rarely, if ever, happens spontaneously in the childhood years; it happens in response to an intentional approach from important adults in a way that has sufficient power to create change and healing.

On the other end of the spectrum of intensity is the so-called 'normal' child—the one who will still engage with life with gusto to see which actions will translate to energized relationship but who will probably subsume the desire to break rules or otherwise act out to achieve the high-end responses. She controls this tendency even as she observes that juicy connection and relationship seem readily available to classmates through adversarial choices. This observation does register with the average or normal child, but he has the ability to call up this pattern of acting-out only as needed. He is the understudy, prepared to leap into the fray. Even the very best children have moments when their intensity/life force spikes to a level that exceeds their internal ability to handle what they are experiencing. We all get needy and difficult from time to time.

No amount of reasoning, logic, punishment, lecturing or moralizing is going to dissuade a child from acting out as long as he believes, based on the truth of his past experiences, that misbehavior is the best way to satisfy his energetic account. Almost *any* response to his poor choices and bad behavior reads energetically as a reward. The exception: a consequence that withdraws connection and energy in response to bad behavior. In the Nurtured Heart Approach, we accomplish this through a brief, un-energized *reset*.

The Reset: A Brief Introduction

A truly effective consequence has a dual effect: it interrupts the pattern of misbehavior, and it has a longer term teaching effect that moves the child forward to a place where poor choices lose their appeal.

In the Nurtured Heart Approach, we use one type of consequence when rules are broken: the reset. You can call it a time-out, a pause, a chill pill, or a break, but no matter what term you use, it is a time-out from connectivity, relationship and interaction that lasts no more than a minute or so but can be over in two seconds flat as well. The reset is covered in depth in Chapter 6.

This is where people get confused and doubtful. *How can I not give energy to negativity and still hold kids accountable?* At one of my presentations, one teacher raised her hand and said, "I have this kid in my kindergarten class who hits and curses at his classmates. How is something that seems like nothing going to have an impact? When parents call me to find out how I'm handling this, do you expect me to tell them I'm giving this child a *10-second reset?*"

"Yes," I told her, and this is why: because *anything else reinforces that child's impression that he gets more out of life through negativity.* More energy poured into dealing with that child's misbehavior is more fuel on that very fire. This teacher, by committing to change the unruly kindergartner's impression that he has to act out to create relationship, will have a true effect on the child's choices about how to behave in the classroom.

To this child, escalating consequences will only read as a reward. They will lead to more hitting and more cursing. A *true* consequence, on the other hand, removes any inkling of the reward of adult energy and connection in response to misbehavior. If a 10-second reset works better to stop the hitting and cursing than the usual laundry list of so-called consequences, why wouldn't that parent on the phone want you to use it?

The power of this consequence has nothing to do with its length. Rather, the substantial power of the reset comes from *refusing to accidentally energize negativity* while simultaneously and with determination illuminating the *greatness* of the moments that follow.

Most people can juggle one ball right away. Most can juggle two within a few minutes. But nobody picks up three balls and starts juggling the first time trying, no matter how athletically gifted he or she might be. In learning and applying the Nurtured Heart Approach, there will be three 'balls' you'll learn to juggle by getting them into the air one at a time. We call them Stands, and they are critical to the approach. Once the first two Stands are 'in the air,' the third Stand—the reset—will slide right into play in a seamless way. If you don't get the first two balls in the air before adding the third, the approach will not work. But when you do get all three of those balls aloft and flying, you'll see how the reset fits perfectly into the overall magic you're creating.

If this "toy story" makes sense to you, and if you're not wanting to be the kind of toy that reactively moves into gear in an energized way when things go wrong, here is the very first move to make to invoke the change you are seeking.

The First Stand: Refuse to Energize Negativity

Many teachers find that a handful of energy-extracting students are basically running the show in a way that disrupts the classroom over and over again. These teachers can end up putting out disciplinary fires instead of teaching. If this describes your classroom, ask yourself: Are you ready to stop letting your difficult students run the show? What do you really want to give your energy to?

It's time to go *with* the current instead of against it. If you are, indeed, the metaphorical favorite toy of every child in your classroom, take advantage of this by **reprogramming your game board so that your most interesting responses and juiciest connection with students come** *in response to positive choices.* With this same reprogramming, the buttons that once made rule-breaking and acting out so exciting and rewarding to students will suddenly yield little or nothing. Pushing those buttons will get very, very boring. **For now, the very first and most vital step is a shift to a stance of** *refusing to give the gift of your aliveness in exchange for negativity.*

Stand #1:
Refuse to Energize Negativity
("Absolutely NO!")

To adopt the first Stand, set an intention to absolutely refuse to give students any energy or emotion when they attempt to gain connection through negative or inappropriate behaviors. "I absolutely will not energize this negativity" is a useful 'mantra' for adopting this stand.

Surrendering Negativity

Take a look at the synonyms listed for the word "negative" below. Do they describe how you want to be in your classroom or in the world in general? Is any of this what you want to give your energy to? **Of course not.**

Synonyms for Negative

Adverse, against, annulling, antagonistic, anti-, balky, colorless, contrary, counteractive, cynical, denying, detrimental, disallowing, disavowing, dissentient, dissenting, gainsaying, gloomy, impugning, invalidating, jaundiced, naysaying, neutralizing, non-affirmative, nullifying, opposing, pessimistic, privative, recusant, refusing, rejecting, repugnant, resisting, resistive, unenthusiastic, unfavorable, uninterested, unwilling, weak

But in practice, this is exactly what we tend to do: give our energy to the negative. When we remain silent and unengaged in the classroom when things are going well, only to pour on the relationship and connection when things go wrong, we are giving our energy to negativity.

When students try to hook you in with inappropriate behaviors, remind yourself: *I am taking a stand. I'm not going there anymore.* **Absolutely NO!**

Disengage the gift that is you. Save your soul for the good stuff—and, as you'll see in the next chapter, there's an incredible abundance of good stuff to be found, even in a classroom full of difficult students. In chapters to come, you will learn to see the incredible array of greatness that's always there to access. You'll learn ways to radically appreciate, radiate recognition and glow in gratitude.

The next stand will show you how to replace that limit-pushing addiction with an attraction to accomplishment, to success and to greatness.

Relationship Is Not Optional

If you do not provide positive relationship with students, they will find a way to access relationship from you by any means necessary, even if it's negative. The good news is that you can make a choice to intentionally, consciously create those positively energized relationships instead of defaulting into the standard pattern of accidentally energizing negativity. And the great news is that this positive realm is endlessly spacious, with room for level upon level of greatness.

It's time to find a new way to have relationships with students that feed their energetic need in a way that serves their souls and brings their greatness to the forefront. We can *revamp ourselves* to be 'toys' that refuse to energize negativity. We can choose instead to energize the positive aspects of students' behaviors and the intrinsic greatness that is expressed in those behaviors.

With this approach, we don't have to answer the question of *why* a child is pushing limits. It's inconsequential, and all the mining for causes tends to work against the Stand of refusing to give energy to negativity. Exploring for "why" essentially gives further evidence to the child that his problems and issues captivate adults the most—that we are most alive, energized and present for problems. As long as a child continues to perceive that he gets more out of adversity than out of success, no 'normal' (read: energetically upside-down) method for getting that child to behave will work.

At Cooley Middle School, principal Karen Calkins advises her teachers, "Don't talk the problem out with the child." What do you do instead? Find a way to shine that bigger light of your heart on the child's success in the very next moments when the problems aren't happening. You'll learn some techniques for doing so in the next chapter. *But what about the problems? We can't just let them go unaddressed,* you might think. Rest assured that when you fail to give your energy to problems, they tend to solve themselves.

"I remember my frustration with Karen [Calkins] before I discovered the Nurtured Heart Approach," school psychologist Mary Martin told me. "I'd think to myself, 'Isn't she going to TALK to that kid about this?! This is NOT okay!' But Karen wouldn't go there." She knew that there was nothing to be gained by going down that slippery slope.

Think of the addict going back to his drug of choice for the hit of energy it offers him. The best way to break that addiction is to remove the energy from the equation. By refusing to energize negativity, you will help your difficult students break what amounts to an addiction: an addiction to pushing limits. You will be refusing to accidentally communicate that you enjoy problems; that you find adversity exciting and compelling; and as energy gets translated in the moment, that you essentially *love* disrespect and rule-breaking.

Energetically congruent messages of loving greatness are ready to be shipped your way. Are you ready?

Notching it Up!
An Approach for Every Student

As the Nurtured Heart Approach was shown to shift hyperactive children to patterns of success, every level of difficult child came my way. People were referring delinquents, gang kids, kids on substances, kids from psychiatric facilities—kids who were turning the world upside down. The approach was up to the task, no matter what problems the child had. The dial could be notched up again and again to whatever level it took to reach even the toughest children.

However, *the Nurtured Heart Approach works for the energy-challenged child in the classroom only when it's used consistently for the entire class* (even better, throughout the entire school; see Chapter 8).

Often, teachers try the approach because they are desperate for something that will help with their few intense and difficult children, but when they end up using the approach with the whole class, every child benefits. When the teacher sees that the intensity with which she applies the approach has to match the intensity of the worst troublemakers, and when she ramps up to that level, classroom discipline issues become almost nonexistent. Energy-challenged children set the bar high; in this context, they're a great blessing. The most difficult child in your classroom serves as a catalyst to dramatically improve the school experience of all of your students. The worst kid becomes one of the best, and everyone else gets to go along on the beautiful ride to greatness.

The result of the reign of terror by the challenging child—more relationship, more positive attention in response to bad behavior—is marketed right there in the classroom. (This is why Individual Education Plans often backfire.) In a class with a difficult child, the cooperative children are already privately miffed that this student is getting away with acting-out and causing pervasive anxiety in the class. They are guarded and angry that the teacher is not handling the child in a way that feels right and effective. And they are utterly aware of the inequities. If you apply any positive approach with the misbehaving child alone, the gap will widen; the inequities will be that much more blatant.

Marginal kids are the understudies. They're taking mental notes as difficult kids get a disproportionate chunk of the prize in the classroom—relationship with the educator. It may not be long before they cross over to become one of the most difficult students.

With a classroom full of well-behaved kids, a mild application of the approach will have huge benefit. If you're dealing with several difficult children (or a classroom full of them), however, you'll need to pump up the basic approach until the intensity of the approach meets the intensity of even the most challenging of your students. Applying it effectively in tough situations is not about making it more complex, but about *holding fast to the model's simplicity while applying it with greater intensity according to what is needed: notching it up.*

To the degree that the approach's aims are achieved through the challenges posed by these intense children, the ability to help all the other children flourish will be multiplied. And you'll stop living in fear of having challenging children in your classroom.

Can you imagine hoping for a doozy of a difficult child next year? I've heard teachers who have bought into this approach expressing this exact hope because they know it will take their creative juices to the next level.

All children have intensity to some degree. We call upon our intensity and life force in everything we do. Without it, we would not be able to live our dreams, fulfill our purposes or accomplish what we desire. We'd have trouble just getting out of bed. Even the best-behaved children have moments when their intensity percolates beyond their wherewithal to handle it. Don't we all? It's through highly intense and challenging children that we can see most clearly how children perceive energy and relationship. This lens reveals what's needed for the more moderate or mild intensity of every other child in a school building.

In many cities in the U.S., the rate of student attrition is over 50 percent, meaning that half of all those beginning public education in kindergarten are not finishing high school. Our current situation might appropriately be labeled "every other child left behind." We are told the dropout rate is 15 percent, but the rate of attrition reflects the real truth of the disenchantment and disenfranchisement to so many.

Rather than bringing back the belt, the whip or the yardstick, it's time to reshape our determination, fierceness and tenacity into an approach that plays hardball from a different vantage point and to apply it to every child with whom we come in contact.

Chapter 3
Time-In! Expect, Create and Reflect Success

Get to the kid's greatness before the kid has a chance to give in to negativity.
—Cooley Middle School principal Karen Calkins

WHEN I VISIT SCHOOLS, I'm usually taken first to a classroom that's in total chaos so I can see what they're dealing with. And next, I observe a room blessed with a teacher who is considered to be highly positive.

The chaotic rooms are no big deal for me—usually, they serve as inspiration for my upcoming presentation to the staff. My biggest frustrations stem from those "highly positive" classrooms. When I visit those rooms, I usually do hear a lot of praise going on. I hear lots of iterations of and variations on "good job," "great job" and "thanks." Once in a while, some detail gets tacked on, like: "Good job staying in your seat!" "Thanks for being quiet." "Way to be focused."

If you were to imagine what your loved ones might say about you in your eulogy, do they extol you for having been good at sitting still in class? Do they say that you were quiet until you were called on? Sat in your chair until dismissal? Stayed focused on your tasks? Never caused a fuss about anything? These would hardly be fitting tributes to your intrinsic greatness as an individual. They are not about how brave or thoughtful, how loving or powerful, how strong or judicious, how compassionate or clear you are. They don't reflect your qualities of approachability, collaborativeness, intelligence or fairness. They don't touch the depth of your determination nor the inspiration or wisdom you offer. They are about behaving yourself—about a mechanical way of being in the world that is all about not being bothersome. That's not who you *really* are.

Who are you, really? You're a unique soul, with a constellation of great qualities like those named above. And those are the qualities you're going to learn to see and describe in your students in this book.

Now that you've taken a stand to refuse to energize negativity, the door is wide open for you to recognize all that's right, passionately and in vivid detail. You probably feel some resistance coming up on this front, and that's normal—our culture often discourages celebration of the positive at the level you are about to be exposed to. Rest assured, though, that so far, I've received not a single report that the use of this approach to cultivate what I call *inner wealth* has caused harm to anyone.

Inner Wealth: An Introduction

Children who are exposed to this approach through parents, teachers or therapists are transformed through the growth of their inner wealth. Inner wealth can be characterized as a 'default setting' in which the person:

- has a vision of himself as successful
- feels able to handle and learn from failures
- has a comfortable relationship (or even a loving relationship) with his own intensity—his life force
- is able to find and maintain presence in any situation
- appreciates beauty
- can handle strong feelings
- can freely give of himself to others with the knowledge that this does not deplete, but rather fortifies
- can live courageously, feeling valued and enjoying everyday life

A child with abundant inner wealth knows she doesn't have to act out or break rules to get what she needs from life. She wants to take good care of her body, mind and spirit; trusts her intuition; and knows she is lovable and meaningful. She tells the truth and possesses wonder, awe, trust, faith and purpose. She feels and lives from her own core of greatness and appreciates the greatness of others.

Is inner wealth self-esteem? Not exactly. I rarely use the term self-esteem anymore. At its roots, self-esteem is about having a stable inner sense of worth: feeling like you have a place in the world, like you're successful, important and necessary. All of these elements are part of inner wealth. But inner wealth has a broader swath and a deeper, more heartful meaning. It's about a child developing faith in herself as intrinsically great—as being meant to live out greatness—and seeing this intrinsic greatness in others as well. This faith comes through repeated experiences of being held in greatness by important people in her life. These people repeatedly energize this child for what she is doing right, which in turn enhances her self-concept as a thriving, successful, capable person.

Some methods to build self-esteem in students recommend "100 ways to praise a child" (if you have that list, get your shredder ready) or the practice in children's sports where everyone gets a trophy, whether they win or lose. **A child has no way of relating generic words of praise ("Great job! Terrific! Wonderful! Good job! Beautiful work!") or a generic trophy to any *specific aspect* of his or her own greatness.** Empty, non-specific words of praise fail to ignite a child's sense of herself as a valuable, participating, successful being. It's the immediacy and specificity of praise that makes it meaningful to a child:

"You're being great right now, and here's exactly how." The Nurtured Heart Approach is a technology that helps adults craft more meaningful and detailed praise, which in turn creates inner wealth. As that happens, so does transformation.

Expressing one-dimensional approval to a child for positive behaviors or rapid-firing one or more of the '100 ways to praise a child' do not provide apt tribute to the compelling constellation of qualities that make each child who and what he or she is in the dance of life. A real tribute has the texture and magnitude to touch a child's heart, bringing renewal and inspiration as he goes forward in life. It would be resolute, clear and resonant in a way that calls him to further greatness. It would have the pixels—the 'zooming in' and detail— that reflect any and every increment of success and that make a compliment irrefutable and powerful.

Imagine the difference for this child who wasn't being a bother if he were appreciated in the following way: "Billy, I appreciate the thoughtfulness you used when you chose not to bother the other students. You could have annoyed them with the chalky eraser. It looked like you were thinking of it, but you exercised good control and great judgment and decided it wasn't a powerful choice. I commend you for your wisdom."

I know, I know. People don't talk like this. *You* don't talk like this. But all you're doing here is making a conscious choice to wax poetic *not about what's going wrong, but about what's going right.*

As weird and quirky as it may initially feel, every time I take my realm of positive statements to some higher level, I am in awe of the reception and resonance it has with others. There's never a problem with the way these out-of-the-ordinary statements are received; the difficulty lies in getting used to expressing myself in this new way!

Have you ever met a child who made poor choices, used poor judgment, had a lack of wisdom and was not thoughtful? If so, you know that it's really not so great to be in his company. So when this child is NOT exhibiting these qualities, even if it happens rarely, we need to give credit when credit is due! There's so much more greatness available to applaud beyond what normally meets the eye.

In the next two chapters, you'll learn four techniques that will give you the ability to weave webs of highly energized appreciation around every student in your classroom. I like to think of these comments as far from ordinary praise; rather, as *radical appreciations.* They go beyond simple descriptiveness—which is what many positive approaches recommend—by making children feel deeply valued, meaningful and noticed. They are designed to transport students into feeling important at the level of the heart.

Notch it Up: *Raise Praise to Encouragement*

Dan Peterson, a counselor in Naperville, Illinois, and a Nurtured Heart Advanced Trainer, makes a great distinction between *praise* and *encouragement*. This distinction suggests that what we're doing in the Nurtured Heart Approach is more aptly described as the latter than the former:

> **Praise** *is given as an external reward for meeting someone else's expectations. It is more about your feelings as the adult whose child has just done something to please you. The focus is more on the result or outcome than on the effort it took to get there. The motivation for the child is limited to times during which you are present. When you leave, the child's motivation to continue to engage in the positive behavior leaves, too.*

> **Encouragement**, *on the other hand, focuses on effort, commitment and dedication to the task rather than to the end result. It assures the child of his value and competence, which leads to a clearer self-awareness and stronger, more positive self-concept. Encouragement inspires a child's desire to use his abilities for the common good, no matter who's watching.*

> *An example of praise would be: "Way to go! You are such a nice kid. Thanks for cleaning up!" An example of encouragement: "I see that you remembered to put your dishes away without being told. You showed your ability to remember the things you've been practicing. You are also showing your independence by doing things without being asked." In the former, the focus is on the result and your feelings about it; the latter statement is all about the child's effort and character—his ability to use his gifts, described in specific detail. With encouragement, you're helping the child internalize evidence that supports his success.*

> *Imagine yourself as a mirror. A mirror doesn't judge or evaluate; it reflects exactly what it sees.*

In this book and in my trainings, I most often reference this as recognition, acknowledgment and appreciation. I rarely use the term 'praise,' but when I do, I'm referring to a notched-up kind of praise—specific, reflective, precise and tailored exactly to the person who's being praised—that fits Dan's definition of encouragement.

Creating a Vibrant 'Time-In' with Highly Energized Recognition

Another way to understand this is that the techniques for radically appreciating students serve the purpose of creating *time-in*. The time-in is when:

- Students are 'in the game'—they are, for the moment, doing the right things and not the wrong things. This sense of being in the game is energetically congruent, not upside-down.

- Students are actively accruing evidence of their qualities of greatness and building inner wealth and a renewed sense of aliveness that is based on this energetic congruence.

- Students come to feel connection and relationship on the basis of *who they are*—collaborative, contributing people in this world that unfolds in the classroom and in the school community.

- Breaking rules and acting out lose their allure because doing the opposite is giving them all the juicy connection they need.

The usual praise offered to children lacks specificity and energy. If praise were a food, 'good job' and 'thanks' might smell good, but they'd lack nutrition. Words like *recognition, encouragement* and *appreciation* are more substantial—akin to a 'meal' more packed with emotional, spiritual and psychological nutrition.

The difference between standard disciplinary approaches and the Nurtured Heart Approach is comparable to the difference between the average American diet and the kind of diet nutrition guru Andrew Weil, M.D., might recommend. In both cases, one buys food, prepares it, chews it and swallows it, but there's a huge quantitative difference in the level of nutrition provided.

Negative attention is like junk food. It has calories but no nutritional value. It downloads as failure and makes the child weaker on the inside. When a child has an accumulation of experiences that he perceives as failures, even if they're simply a continual stream of critiques or attempted limit-setting ("Cut it out!" "Stop it!" "Quit it!"), he becomes immune to the comments that are continually flung his way, tuning in solely to the energetic subtext (misbehavior = relationship) beneath those words. He also stops being moved by normal praise because he develops an inner image of himself as a kid who couldn't possibly be good. By giving the child reflections of what's actually transpiring when he is *not* going down the road of negativity, and by learning to reflect all the positives woven into the texture of the truth of those moments, we provide excellent emotional and psychological nutrition.

Normal recognition tends to be under-energized and vague. Being told "thanks" or "good job" often means "you're falling in line" and nothing more. For a child who has been stuck in the upside-down pattern we've described herein, these kinds of compliments are like being told "You look nice!" on a day that you don't feel you look nice. You need compelling supporting evidence to believe this compliment. Try going around your classroom offering vague comments like "Way to go!" or "Excellent" or "Wonderful," the type of words typically used to praise students. Although the intention to approve and compliment is present, if you watch the faces of the children closely, you'll likely see that although they seem to like it, they have no idea what you are recognizing. Normal praise is no match for the energy we convey when things are going wrong, at which point our responses and reactions become exacting, charged and eloquent in their detail of the situation's wrongness.

In contrast, capturing a child's moment of success and vividly verbalizing it, you send information past the child's defenses. **You are *confronting* the child in a great new way with the message: "Here you are, being successful! It's not a question of whether you can or can't, you *are*!"**

Stand #2:
Relentlessly Energize the Positive ("Absolutely YES!")

When a student is doing something right or is *not* doing something wrong, you can offer a message that translates energetically to "absolutely YES!" Being relentless on this front is about demonstrating to students that you're not going to go down the road of energizing negativity—because you have so much to energize on the positive side of things. This Stand goes hand-in-hand with Stand 1, where you resolutely refuse to energize negativity.

Through this mantra/inner declaration of YES, you're saying "absolutely yes" to creating even more opportunities to say to students: Yes, you *are* doing the right thing and *not* the wrong thing; yes, you are valued and meaningful.

Video Games and Time-In

The best analogy I've found to describe time-in and this commitment to YES relies on something a lot of parents and teachers would rather kids do without: video games. When I use this analogy, the adults in the room tend to experience an "aha" moment where everything seems to make perfect sense.

What is it, exactly, that makes these games so compelling? Why can a child who seems constitutionally unable to sit still for three minutes in a classroom be completely engrossed for hours on end in one of these games? Kids don't just play these games, they play them to win. They play them with fascinated mastery and an authentic desire for achievement.

Most children who become intrigued by the prospects of these games want to leapfrog to the highest levels possible. Most parents, even if they resent the insanity, the bizarre content or the violence of these games, at least admire the games' ability to hold their child's attention. Many wonder why their child can't go after real-life successes in the same tenacious manner.

Here's one possible explanation of what sets kids so free to play with such zeal and inspiration. **While playing a video game, a child's life makes sense in a way that doesn't carry over into real life.**

In the game, as long as the rules are followed and appropriate point-gar-nering actions are happening, points accrue and the player moves from level to level. There's consistent, instantaneous positive reinforcement for success as reflected by the accrual of points and other engaging feedback as one plays. Success is communicated vividly and immediately through an energetic ex-change as long as the game is going well. This is time-in at its best. The default setting of the game is to YES. The game relentlessly returns to success.

At the same time, video games refuse to energize rules broken and mistakes made. Most games give a predictable response whenever you err. Once you've erred enough times, you're out. But you need only endure what amounts to a brief pause from the action—long enough to reset to the next moment of suc-cess or to the next game to start over.

When the child breaks a rule in the game, it doesn't say, "Oh, please don't do that anymore!" or "Make better choices from now on!" Consequences are immediate and don't vary according to circumstances. The accrual of points and the energizing of success stop momentarily but then resume as the player gets two or three more chances to jump back into the game. And as long as the rules are followed, he can continue to collect points and get all the positive recognition the game offers. With each new game, the player is faced with the same vast possibilities for success.

After suffering a few moments of being out of the loop and missing out on the game's payoffs, the child comes back with even more tenacity to not break rules. No one is twisting his arm. Of his own volition, he is determined to avoid breaking the rules of the game. Although to adults the consequences for break-ing rules might seem punitive and drastic, the child realizes that, despite all that gore and blood and those cataclysmic explosions, the video game conse-quence is, basically, *nothing*. He sees that he can easily fulfill the consequence's requirements and that he's back in the game in a matter of seconds. He comes to trust that moving back into the game's default setting is easy and that this setting is always accessible. As the game energetically confronts his successes with consistency, he's motivated to redouble his determination to find further success and to beat the last round's score.

The video game consequence is *an illusion*, but its absolute *clarity* plays into the child's reaching for higher and higher levels of greatness. It works because the time-in established by the game is so compelling and predictable. No child plays video games to lose. These games waltz the child into an inner framework of mastery and accomplishment.

When adults learning this approach are advised that rule-breaking should be answered only with a brief, un-energized reset, they are usually skeptical that this could possibly be an effective deterrent or consequence. But this video game logic helps plant the seed of possibility that somehow, someway, the short consequence might work.

Later we will delve into the consequence of reset in detail. For now, the important and illuminating piece of this analogy is this: the momentary reset, this illusion of a consequence, is only effective because the game is so alive in its energetic rendition of success. In other words, **being out of the loop for even a few seconds gives the child a tremendous feeling of missing out and wanting to be back in the game.** The energetic excitement engendered by the game's default setting to success actually creates something to miss out on— and subsequently, not only a quest to get back, but to get back in and tenaciously seek ever greater levels.

The brevity of the consequence/reset used in this approach (two seconds to a minute at most) fits into this video game logic, too. If the time-out/reset that takes place when a child loses in a video game is too long, the child is likely to lose interest and walk away from the game. Similarly, a consequence that's too long works against a major aim of the approach: to convince students that time-in is always within their grasp. The reset leads back in an airtight way to a default setting of success. It hijacks the child back into this radically appreciative realm, again and again.

When you refuse to energize negativity while both relentlessly energizing positivity and holding clear accountability, you create a time-in that strongly resembles the state a child experiences while playing a video game. They start to play the game of life with similar zeal.

Setting Your Intention: Prepare to Be Tested

Intention is defined as 'a determination to act in a certain way; what one intends in order to accomplish or attain.' For me, intention is also *what one intends to hold as true.* It's a guiding clarity that supports the pursuit and purpose of that attainment. These Stands are, at their foundation, *intentions.*

This becomes crucial as you begin to demonstrate to the children in your life that things have changed and that you have shifted your style of relating to them. You will be challenged by children as you undertake this endeavor. Testing is part of the job description of any child, and it's in this challenging and testing that the child learns that your energetic connection can no longer be had through negativity. When this happens, you might be tempted to back down.

Instead, we urge you to see it as your big opportunity to dig in—to *notch it up*. Remind yourself that you are taking a stand for new ways of creating impact that will lead these children to their greatness.

If you begin to use these techniques and one of your students says, "Did you learn some new trick to try to keep us in line or something?" remember this: *you are taking a stand.* Your response might be: "I'm honored that you see that I'm doing something different. It's not a trick. I realized I was great at being critical and pointing out what you all do wrong, but not so great at recognizing everything you do right. I'm changing that around. Thanks for asking. I appreciate your curiosity." Meta-message: this isn't going away. And in the process of not backing down and running for the hills because a child sees 'through you,' you wind up providing even more recognition and appreciation. Let's call it an alternative way of playing hardball—with intention.

As you align with the Stands in this book, take time to acknowledge to yourself how you are connecting intention with action—an indication of great discipline, tenacity, commitment to your students and ability to follow through!

The chapters that follow cover four specific methods for upholding the second Stand. Any time those methods begin to feel rote, false or forced, or any time you encounter resistance from students or peers, remember that as an educator, you best serve your students by bringing out and burnishing their intrinsic greatness. You now know that difficult children can be transformed only if the traditional upside-down energy is emphatically turned back to right-side-up through positive recognition. This book will give you the tools to do that.

Keep resetting to your own greatness, adhering to the two Stands and expressing your unique self through these tools. Soon it will feel as natural as breathing.

Notching it Up!
A Spiritual Approach

You've read about a third of this book already and I haven't offered you a single concrete technique that you can take into the classroom. *"Come on, Howard, land the plane,"* you might be thinking.

In my trainings, this is where participants start to get really impatient. They've listened to me go on and on about energy and negativity and toys and they're ready for some techniques already. They are eager to apply the insights they're having to the children in their lives.

Until you thoroughly grasp the intentions behind the techniques, they'll be just that: techniques. And your students will know that you're just trying some new technique so they'll behave. Here, we're exiting the screen labeled 'behavior management' and moving into the realm that I like to think of as a spiritual intervention. We'll get to techniques in the next chapter, but a deep understanding of the approach's intentions will make their application much more fulfilling, powerful and intuitive.

The most important of these intentions is to accept that *every one of us has greatness that can be awakened.* Living this approach is about knowing that, in any moment, we can choose to see, reflect and acknowledge greatness—that ordinary moments can be transformed into extraordinary moments.

Learning to see what's great in others and in yourself is, I daresay, a spiritual experience. If you were to wake up tomorrow to a renewed ability to see compassionately, characterized by more generosity, synergy and clarity about your own greatness and the greatness of others, wouldn't that be a spiritual experience? If you woke up with a deeper and more abiding truth about that greatness, wouldn't that be a spiritual experience that might ripple out into your life and impact others?

This approach can work if it's just "done" as a set of techniques. But notching it up requires a deep and heartfelt understanding of the approach's intentions—a spiritual shift that leads to many "aha" moments.

Chapter 4

Seeing and Acknowledging What's Right: Active and Experiential Recognitions

The techniques we use to fulfill Stand 2 are founded on a few more of those simple notions I came up with all those years ago. You'll find these notions interwoven with the descriptions of the techniques throughout this chapter.

Are these techniques about 'catching kids being good?' No. Please think of me as the guy who's *against* catching kids being good. If you're in a room with a challenging child and waiting for him to do something good, you are completely at the mercy of what might or might not happen. Waiting for a challenging child to be good can feel like trying to catch a dinosaur in a butterfly net. *Not* the right tool for the job—I don't ever want to be that disempowered! I want to have exquisite positive impact in a room full of kids, and to do that, I need a bigger net.

I want to know how to *create* a child being great by the way I construe him in any given moment. I want methods that will enable me to point out success when *I* choose to do so—so that at any time I choose, I can say, "You *are* being great, and here's exactly how you're being great, right now." I want to see and say things in a way that will multiply the impact of my words. I want to be able to find success in both what *is* happening, as well as in what *isn't* happening.

We're looking for ways to be positive that *get around a child's defenses*. With any child, and especially with an energy-challenged child, we must convey that he has really and truly been seen and appreciated—that we are not just complimenting him to get him to behave. The burden of proof is on us to give recognitions that are authentic, real and energetically congruent with the situation and with the truth of who the child is in that moment. Defenses can be quite strong; getting under the radar is crucial.

Like the Stands, these techniques build upon each other; **in the end you will use them all interchangeably and in your own unique way**. It can be helpful, however, to apply one technique for a few days before moving on and building in the next one. Fit the methods to your own individual style.

First Technique: Active Recognition

Offer a 'verbal snapshot' or sound bite of what a student is doing as though you were describing it to a blind person. Shine the light of your awareness on what a child is doing in a way that makes the child feel acknowledged. Rattle off what you see in your mental "Kodak moment." This conveys to the child: "You're valuable and meaningful to me." It's a great way of playing hardball with the intention of "*yes*" as it conveys deeply that the child is seen, noticed and appreciated. It is the "yes" of attunement.

Be honest. Never lie. You don't need anything stunning, just the everyday living of the child. Ordinary actions, emotions and moments are all windows of opportunity. Remain intent on reporting what you see and reserving this narration for when things are *not* going wrong. Remember the horse whisperer: "It's not a question of whether you can or you can't—you *are*."

I often tell the story of a toll-taker on a toll bridge to underline the power that intention gives to this and other techniques.

> From a distance, a commuter arriving at the San Francisco Bay Bridge one Saturday morning sees one tollbooth attendant who appears to be dancing—not just bopping a little side to side, but moving and grooving in his booth. As traffic is light, the driver is able to maneuver his way into the dancing toll-taker's lane.
>
> Loud music pours out of the tollbooth's window, and the driver sees that yes, indeed, this tollbooth attendant is dancing his heart out. As they make their transaction, the driver says, "Wow, you look like you're enjoying yourself."
>
> "That's right!" says the toll-taker. "This is the best job ever. I can listen to my tunes. I have incredible views in every direction. I get to talk to nice people all day. And best of all, I get to exercise and practice my moves while I work and earn a salary—I'm studying to be a professional dancer."
>
> The driver points out the adjacent attendants, who look far less thrilled to be at their posts. "What about them?" the driver asks. "They don't seem to think this is the best job ever."
>
> "Oh, them?" the toll-taker replies. "Those guys in the stand-up coffins? They're no fun."

We get to choose how we perceive the world. Whether you see the glass as half full or half empty, you are making a choice. Whether you see yourself or another as a raving success or as miserably flawed, you are making the choice to see through a lens of your choosing. The glass is always filled to exactly the level of your intention.

Accept the responsibility and power inherent in recognizing that you get to choose how you perceive and envision your world. You can *hold an intention to see what's positive.* **Holding the intention to keep resetting to greatness is the foundation of the Nurtured Heart Approach.**

We have a choice, *in every single moment,* in how we see the world around us. It's always our choice, and our intentions guide and inspire us in continually honing each next now.

Here's what I recommend to start the ball rolling—a ball that can truly accelerate now that there's no longer energy for negativity. See—really *see*—everyday actions and emotions and reflect them back verbally. This will demonstrate to students that they are noticed, meaningful and cherished. This is a 'reporting' style of appreciation because you are merely reporting your observation, not passing judgment. The message gets through any defensiveness, hitting home because the texture of the recognition's detail makes it irrefutable.

Although simply reporting what you see might not seem like much recognition, know that *children translate this form of being seen and valued as being successful.* This style of recognition gives you the blank pages to begin authoring the accumulation of inner wealth.

This technique puts you in the driver's seat, actively creating successes by choosing to see success in the very act of the child living his or her life. Inherent in this simple technique is a stance that allows you to be a warrior—relentlessly, if needed, conveying interest, caring and love to the child without having to wait for high-profile successes to come along.

Part of the sweetness of this technique, and something that you will soon see, is that this act of profound attunement energetically conveys love, kindness, compassion and caring without your ever having to say that this is what you are feeling or doing. You will see the child's heart open to your words. And if it remains closed, don't worry—all you need to do is notch it up.

Many children enter adulthood with a belief that their only true value comes with high-level achieving; they find themselves flip-flopping between stressful pursuits of the impossible and feelings of failure and resentment. Children who receive empty, non-specific praises by the truckload—"you're awesome" or "you're terrific" or "you're wonderful and amazing!"—**experience a painful dissonance because they don't get *how* or *why* they are so awesome, terrific, wonderful and amazing.** Active Recognitions convey that every child is meaningful and valued not just for high-level achievements, but also for their simple yet specific everyday ways of being.

A Different Slant on High Expectations

"Why reward mediocrity?" you might be thinking. "All this recognition and appreciation for just doing what kids *should* do? What's to motivate them to aim higher and do more, do better?" By setting a foundation of appreciation for the child's simplest ways of being in the world, we set the stage for the child to meet much higher expectations. They are not inspired to achieve when we accuse them of falling short. Inspiration comes *when we acknowledge how they are being successful.* Having that success acknowledged consistently creates a core sense of successfulness (inner wealth), which powerfully shapes the child's emerging self. This is what we are aiming for: a time-in where success is impossible to avoid.

I'm all for high expectations, but we hang ourselves with them sometimes. So many children come to believe that they can't expect approval or connection from adults unless they achieve some sort of perfection. How much unhappiness and self-flagellation do adults indulge in because they feel they're falling short? How many adults do you know who feel genuinely happy with their accomplishments and with living their sense of purpose—who see their everyday lives as worthwhile and sacred?

In recent decades, many adults have found themselves mired in spiritual crises, depression and anxiety over feelings of not being 'enough' just as they are. Many spiritual practices are about helping us to dis-identify ourselves from our high-achieving expectations and to instead see the beauty of the self that just *is*. This is the steady, naturally joyous self, the fundamentally positive life force that exists beneath all of our mental chatter and emotional ups and downs. Children have ready access to this self, but the world's pressures to achieve separate them from it. This is what happened to most of us by the time we were in our teens.

Wouldn't it be wonderful to show children a way to stay engaged with this fundamental self? This is what Active Recognitions and the other techniques we will describe end up doing: they recognize the child for the inner being and depth of greatness that are every child's birthright. In recognizing this verbally, we show that we see that inner light and appreciate it—and that it's something the child herself can appreciate as well. Detailed recognition and appreciation make that light shine more brightly.

Active Recognitions give you, the educator, a wide set of possibilities to *convey* success. Almost any moment can be seen as an opportunity to communicate value and interest. How empowering! You are the producer, director and editor of all the footage of these moments, and it is always *your* voiceover.

Use neutral, non-judgmental language. Strive to be as specific as possible— give lots of information. Lisa being told that her picture is beautiful won't download as a true, fully convincing or deep experience of success; but if you describe the yellows and blues and greens of her picture and the lines and shapes of her art, she will feel her effort has been truly noticed and appreciated.

Here are a few samples of Active Recognitions:

"Paul, I see that you are using your control to not speak out of turn, even though you looked so tempted."

"Sydney, I see that you are gluing different colors of tissue to your collage. You are creating a lot of texture and depth."

"George, I hear you asking Tina to share her book. You are not just pulling the book away. You are asking with such kindness."

"I notice that Tim, Caroline and Fiona are lining up to go to lunch and getting to their spots in a very collaborative way."

Whether the student is engaged in ordinary or exemplary behavior, this technique can remain neutral; there is no need for judgment or evaluation. Just use as detailed an observation as possible, although some more specific appreciations of good choices can be woven in to fit the situation (you'll see how in the next two techniques).

Do not use this technique to observe a child's actions when those actions are negative. If you say, "I can see that Paul is getting ready to speak out of turn," he is still gaining your energized involvement in response to the poor choice he is making and he will know that. I've seen many educators do this and it makes the situation worse. Only use this technique when problems are not happening. (Later, you'll see how other techniques can be used when a child begins to edge up to a boundary.)

Active Recognition is particularly useful for:

• **Children who are extremely energy-challenged and don't yet digest direct recognition well.** For a child who is used to getting lots of juice from negativity, Active Recognition is a good starting point to nurture a new way of feeling seen and appreciated by adults. It can provide the springboard for working into moments of what's right that might otherwise be lost in the midst of frequent poor choices. It helps open a resistant child to the notion that acting out may no longer be necessary for him to get involvement, connection and relationship, providing incontrovertible proof that he's seen when he is doing *right*, not just when he is doing wrong.

• **Children who are emotionally wound up but who haven't yet acted out.** Active Recognitions are a wonderful way to teach a child that he or she is capable of feeling and handling such strong feelings. The child learns that she is entitled to these feelings and that she has the power to handle them without letting them move her into behaviors that get her into trouble. "Julia, I see that you are feeling upset and frustrated. You are handling your anger so well. It would have been so easy to lash out and fuss, but you chose not to."

Although these kinds of recognition are especially potent for challenging children, often serving as turning points for them, *every* child deserves this kind of notice and credit.

Begin to weave Active Recognitions into your days in the classroom as you teach your curriculum. Start with just a few a day and see what happens. Keep refusing to energize negativity; when it comes up, simply shift your focus to energizing someone in the room who's modeling success. Begin to heighten your appreciation of success being readily available—there for the choosing.

Loud and Clear

At a recent Nurtured Heart training, we used video footage of a great teacher who had mastered the approach in his elementary-school classroom. As he taught, he reflected loud and clear that he'd seen one student turn his chair to face the front of the room for a better view of the lesson. In the next moment, *every single chair* was turned to face the front of the room.

Although private and individual recognitions are part of the flow of a teacher's movements around the room, broadcasting your specific recognitions loudly enough for the whole classroom to hear is a very powerful way to synergize and catalyze the energy of the room. Use modulations in pitch to add texture to this energy.

Second Technique: Experiential Recognition

In practice, those who use the approach don't often use Active Recognitions alone. Crafting them is a good way to begin experimenting with this 'new' language and can help you find ways to start to energize children who strongly resist the second and third techniques. But once you get the hang of it, you'll likely most often add acknowledgements of values or meaningful qualities as demonstrated by whatever the child is doing. You will do this using the second technique, Experiential Recognition.

If you were to approach a table of children who are working together quietly and following all the rules, you could accurately say, "You guys are doing great!" If you went on to ask them *how* they were doing great, however, what might they say? They're not likely to wax poetic about all the values and qualities of greatness they're embodying: "I'm being collaborative! I'm being of assistance, cooperating and sharing materials! I'm being thoughtful with the other kids!" (The exception to this would be the child who has been exposed to the Nurtured Heart Approach; you'll see why in a moment.)

Does any teacher not want his or her students to be respectful? Honest? Responsible? Cooperative? Creative? Decisive? These are precious qualities and values. However, when do we typically bring up these values and qualities? *When the child is NOT embodying them!* In our kind and loving way, we sit the rule-breaker down and lean in. We're so present! There's so much to say! We're riveted. We bring our beings, souls and aliveness to the child in response to behaviors in a way that suggests that a *lack* of desirable qualities is what truly captivates us.

How receptive are children to the lessons we are trying to download when we deliver such lectures and reprimands under these circumstances? Are they open and inspired, or closed and shut down? These attempts to teach values from a problem orientation tend to fall short of their intended mission, and they often deepen the children's impression that they can get more out of life by perpetuating problems.

Character education programs seek to teach values through clever curricula like 'Character Counts!' with its Six Pillars of Character (Trustworthiness, Respect, Responsibility, Fairness, Caring and Citizenship). It's well-intentioned, and many children benefit from this and other such programs—but in the end, these values are abstract notions until a child has someone point out, in the moment, that what he is doing is an expression of one or more of these desirable values. Until such moments, these values are theoretical and philosophical. They do not fully "bake in" until they become first-hand experiences.

Children do not naturally see how their behaviors reflect those qualities. They need our help to download an *experience of themselves* as trustworthy, respectful, responsible, fair, caring, thoughtful and so on. In teaching these values without that direct experience on the child's part, what we end up accidentally communicating is, "Here are some values you should be expressing in your life...but right now, you aren't embodying them." This kind of detached values education fails to teach kids how to live those desirable values.

One teacher told me about an exercise done for Valentine's Day where children filled out cards for all of their classmates that included a compliment. When a child sits down to read a bunch of compliments that aren't grounded in actual experiences, they aren't really absorbed. It's easy for the child to doubt the compliment given in this way, especially in instances when the child's portfolio has been built on negativity.

With Experiential Recognition, we recognize and appreciate the qualities we wish to enhance, specifically and with vivid detail. We teach values in a way that mimics the polishing of a gem: we find a facet and shine the light of our energy on it. We breathe life into these qualities as aspects of this living, breathing child.

Values are defined as qualities of behavior, thought and character that are regarded as intrinsically good and worthy of imitation. They are principles that govern behavior and reflect what's considered to be good, moral and desirable in a culture. With this technique, we teach values through verbal reflections of the child's actual experiences of living those values. Rather than pointing out an instance when a child is *not* exhibiting a value in an effort to instill it via a lecture or a reprimand, we seek out and even *create* opportunities to recognize how a child is embodying values we'd like to encourage. We link Active Recognition of what the child is doing in this moment to the experience of living these positive values.

For example, saying "Jennifer, please be respectful to those at your table…it's not okay to grab what they are working on," however well-intentioned, inadvertently communicates that she is not being respectful and that this is of great interest to you. Instead, seize a moment when Jennifer is *not* grabbing or offending in any other manner and then tell her the truth of that moment so she can have the experience of embodying that quality in a present first-hand moment. "Jennifer, I appreciate how you are sharing the space at your table right now. You are respecting others by giving them room to focus on their work. You are being thoughtful and considerate of others. That shows respect…a great quality." In the former situation, one would accidentally be energetically recognizing Jennifer when she's *not* respectful. In the latter situation, she is getting a glimpse of herself as a person who is capable and honored for doing the right things. The magic is all in our choice of focus.

You can be specifically on the lookout for a quality a student could use a little more of. If Yvette has a tendency to be disrespectful, make a point of recognizing her for being respectful three or four times a day. Or if a certain quality, perhaps being responsible, looms large as a pivotal quality in your thinking, then lobby for blossoming responsibility through this alternative way of pointing it out. There are hundreds of ways of being responsible; you will find many angles in which to tilt the lens of appreciation.

This method can be used to teach academically oriented values, too: "Toby, you're taking lots of time to draw your graph neatly, with a sharp pencil. I love how diligently you work and how attentive to detail you are."

With this approach and this technique, the child is placed squarely in the middle of a story that is about him or herself *being cherished and valued*. Children respond so much better when they irrefutably arrive at the conclusion that they ARE the quality in question, rather than being exposed to it in an abstract way. Instead of saying "You're so smart!" we say "I see your intelligence in this particular thing you are doing."

Let's look at how you might add Experiential Recognitions to the examples of Active Recognitions we listed a few pages earlier in this chapter:

- "Paul, I see that you are using your control to not speak out of turn, even though you looked so tempted." You might add: "That's a great choice you are making right now to use your power and wisdom."

- "Sydney, I see that you are gluing different colors of tissue to your collage. You are creating a lot of texture and depth." You could add, "This shows the great creativity you have and your ability and desire to be artistic and expressive." Or you might say, "Sydney, you're being innovative and expressive—letting that creativity pour right out!"

- "George, I hear you asking Tina to share her book." You might add, "This shows that you care and that is a great quality you have. Your good manners and respect for Tina prove that to me." Another example: "George, that's great assertiveness you're showing! Tina's agreeing to let you look on—Tina, that's a nice demonstration of cooperation and courtesy. You both found a way to be collaborative."

- "I notice that Tim, Caroline and Fiona are lining up to go to lunch and getting to their spots in a very collaborative way." The Experiential Recognition you could add might be: "The way you three are choosing to get along with your classmates shows me you think of others, what they need and what I need, and it shows your desire to be helpful. This great collaboration is so appreciated." Another option would be: "Great forethought and decisiveness—the bell hasn't even rung yet!"

Experiential Recognitions, like Active Recognitions, are particularly nourishing to students when they are in the throes of strong feelings but have not acted out. "Jenny, I see that you are feeling angry at Kim for taking that book away from you without asking. I also see that you are doing everything you can to stay calm and get your book back without aggression. That's real self-control and maturity."

A bit later in this chapter, a list of values is provided for you to draw from for your Experiential Recognitions. (I also like to call these *qualities of greatness*.) Apply this technique in moments when your students are behaving well, and express as much excitement as possible (while still being honest and true to yourself) through your vocal tone and inflection. The power comes from authentically communicating your awareness of all you are appreciating.

Most conventional positive statements don't feel authentic enough to the child, and the caring adults who are trying to apply positive methods sometimes give up when they perceive that the intended compliments are not getting through. In contrast, Experiential Recognitions have enough convincing detail to move past defenses—to pop appreciations directly into the "in-box" instead of getting rejected as spam.

In this movie that is your life, go frame by frame by frame to find and create noteworthy moments for appreciation. As its director, you can choose to stay in your heart and share your gratitude and appreciation for what you see. Moments to recognize are always available. They are boundless, and they are absolutely alive. There's never a shortage of moments to choose from and to frame in any manner you wish. The more conscious of this you strive to be, the more levels of awareness you will find. We are always choosing how we are going to be in each next moment, anyway; let the intention to create success and the gratitude in your heart take the lead.

Miracles from Molecules

Even when a child is having a challenging day, you can find *many* things to get excited about if you're willing to look at the numerous facets and nuances of positive values and behaviors. We can choose to make mountains from molehills—to take small problems and magnify them—or we can choose the opposite: to make miracles from molecules.

We expect ourselves to accomplish certain things each day. For example: you probably expect that you will get a good breakfast into your belly every morning before work. When you manage this, you likely don't go around acknowledging yourself for success, much less greatness. But let's take a closer look at what has to transpire for this everyday expectation to be met.

To get up by six-thirty in the morning, you have to make sure to go to bed at a reasonable hour and do all the self-care necessary to ensure a good night's rest: doing your nightly hygiene; maintaining a pleasant place where you can sleep comfortably; not eating a heavy meal or exercising or watching a stimulating TV show or movie too late at night. You have to remember to set your alarm properly.

In the morning, you have to make decisions about what to wear: Does it match? Is it all clean and free of stains? Is it pressed? You have to take the time and put in the effort to groom yourself. There's shaving, hair care, deodorant or perfume, and makeup if you wear it. And you have to fit all of this in while leaving time for the preparation and consumption of a healthy first meal of the day.

Breakfast time! You have to understand what a healthy breakfast really entails since toaster pastries or a bowl of sugary cereal may not adequately sustain your energy and focus through midmorning. That likely means that you have educated yourself through books, TV shows or other research about what your body needs for breakfast. You had the foresight to grocery shop appropriately to stock your kitchen with all you need to make a healthy breakfast, which in turn requires good management of your time and money.

Let's say you choose to cook scrambled eggs with spinach and two slices of whole-grain buttered toast. A great many steps go into the preparation of this meal. You have to crack the eggs without getting shell bits in the bowl; you have to set the toaster properly to toast without burning; you have to wash your spinach carefully to remove all sand and grit, then chop it without cutting yourself; and you have to pay close attention while cooking the eggs to avoid overcooking or undercooking them. And then, when you sit down to eat, you need to remember to completely chew each bite before swallowing to get more enjoyment out of your wholesome breakfast.

Then there are the dishes to wash and put in the drying rack or dishwasher and the table to be wiped clean. You then need to brush your teeth and make

Values and Qualities Worth Acknowledging

Here is a comprehensive but far from complete list of values and qualities you can begin to use to reflect success to your students.

Abundance	Daring	Good
Acceptance	Dedication	sportsmanship
Accuracy	Depth	Gratitude
Activism	Determination	Guidance
Adaptability	Dignity	Harmony
Adventurous	Discernment	Healing
Affection	Differentiation	Heart
Agility	Discretion	Helpful
Alertness	Efficiency	Honesty
Altruism	Elation	Hope
Articulate	Elegance	Humility
Assertiveness	Empathy	Humor
Attentive	Endurance	Imagination
Awareness	Energetic	Independence
Audacity	Expansiveness	Industry
Balance	Experimentation	Inquisitive
Benevolence	Fairness	Intelligence
Boldness	Faith	Insight
Candor	Fearless	Integrity
Clarity	Ferocity	Intensity
Cleverness	Fidelity	Intuition
Collaboration	Flexibility	Joy
Compassion	Flow	Justice/
Confidence	Focus	being just
Connection	Forethought	Kindness
Conscientious	Forgiveness	Knowledge
Caring	Friendship	Laughter
Consideration	Frugality	Leadership
Cooperation	Fun	Loving
Courage	Generosity	Loyalty
Courtesy	Good judgment	Mastery
Curiosity	Good manners	Mindfulness

Observing	Respect	Thoughtful
Open-minded	Responsibility	Thrift
Open	Restraint	Tolerance
Organization	Reverence	Tranquility
Originality	Sacrifice	Unflappability
Passion	Security	Unity
Patience	Self-control	Unique
Peaceful	Self-mastery	Valor
Perceptive	Sensitivity	Vibrancy
Perseverance	Service	Vigor
Perspective	Spirituality	Virtue
Playfulness	Spontaneity	Visionary
Power	Spunk	Warmth
Precision	Stability	Warrior-like
Productive	Stealth	(positive power)
Professionalism	Stillness	Willingness
Reason	Strength	Wisdom
Receiving	Sympathy	Witty
Relaxation	Synergy	Zeal
Resilience	Teamwork	
Resolve	Thorough	

Some of these words might be beyond your students' current level of understanding. Merely simplify the expression of values as needed, or let this be an opportunity to teach your students powerful new words they can use to define their own success. I've seen preschoolers readily learn words like the ones listed above when they are used in compliments and appreciations. The approach creates opportunities to introduce these new words through explanations of whatever nuance of success is being expressed.

In one Head Start classroom in Tucson, Arizona, teachers meet before class to decide on a new value/quality to teach that day through Experiential Recognition. On a day when they learned about integrity, these four- and five-year-olds were accurately pointing it out in their classmates: "Hey, he's showing integrity! He told the truth." As they actually live these values and have that reflected in the moment, students get a much better grasp of what they mean than they would from a standard vocabulary exercise!

sure you don't have any bits of breakfast stuck to your face or clothes. Then you need to make sure you have everything you need for work before heading out to the car with enough time to get to your place of employment.

Even if you don't have time for anything but a bagel and a cup of coffee, all of the minute and seemingly mundane steps this entails can still be broken down and added up to equal success in terms of all you need to bring to the equation for this event to slip into place. Just think of all you needed to do at work today—all your efforts and resourcefulness—to earn the money to simply pay for the apartment where all this takes place, to buy the transportation that makes work possible, and to purchase the bed, pillows, blankets and food, without which this story could never unfold.

Should you have children and domestic partners to account for, multiply the effort by tenfold—as well as the attributes of success that spin out from simply getting everything taken care of in the morning.

As is readily apparent from this everyday tale of turning molecules into miracles, there is ample opportunity for recognition and appreciation in every single moment of our lives and our students' lives, even the most challenging and difficult ones. Any moment can be expanded in this way as you seek evidence of success. There is always something to appreciate. **You're expanding everyday happenings at the molecular level and finding all of the little miracles therein.**

In computer graphics, the word *pixelation* describes a process of enlarging a portion of an image enough that the component *pixels* (which appear as little squares of various colors) are visible. We do this when we make miracles from molecules: we zoom in as closely as necessary to find something to reflect upon in a positive way.

If a child is taking out a textbook as asked, he is keeping up with the lesson, being attentive, being responsive and demonstrating enthusiasm for learning. If she raises her hand to speak, she is demonstrating respect for her classmates and teacher, being thoughtful and considerate, and demonstrating an understanding and acceptance of the rules of the classroom. When your students show up on time, ready to learn, and then get through a school day, they're successful in enough ways to fill an entire chapter of this book.

To break down everyday pursuits in this way requires that you live vividly in the moment and hold that intention to mine out successes. My intention is to *create miracles from molecules*—and that, for me, means taking an ordinary desire to be positive to an unyielding, relentless, unstoppable force to make success happen.

By way of this intention and mindset, I no longer have to worry about finding successes or hoping to "catch" goodness. Now I can creatively dissect moments to unwrap the success that is always there for the taking. I can then disseminate reflections of that success to whomever I choose. And it really is always a matter of choice—no one can stop me when I activate determination. Whatever level of determination I choose to rise to, I generate a corresponding level of creativity.

The present, the 'Now,' is all we have; the past is done, the future unknown. Spiritual teacher Ram Dass exhorted us to "be here now;" I like to take this a step further: to *be here knowing* that it is entirely possible to bring greatness to the moment by expanding everyday tasks and routines to see and recognize students' greatness *right now*. This is pixelation, Nurtured Heart style—knowing what you want to do with the moment and knowing how.

If you can't easily see something on your computer at the present resolution, you zoom in to a more pixelated vantage point. With this approach, do the same: zoom in to find ways to verbally reflect all there is to appreciate.

It's an act of creativity. You are fearlessly *creating* kids being good in the truth of the moment. Know that any time you want, you can *steal* a moment of greatness. Cheating, hijacking, larceny—these words all get a bad rap, but they are appropriate descriptors of this process of making success impossible to avoid. The tougher the kid, the more hijacking you'll have to do.

Restocking the Portfolio

Visual artists and others who need to keep a collection of their work in one place to show to interested parties usually do so in something called a *portfolio*. In my teaching about this approach, I find this word useful as a way to describe a virtual place where we keep all our thoughts, ideas, judgments and feelings about ourselves: who we are, what our value is to the world and how we think others see us. Difficult and energy-challenged children tend to have portfolios filled with negative notions about themselves, along with firmly entrenched ideas about what they need to do in order to be most energetically of interest to and celebrated by others. Through this approach, we can re-load their portfolios with the very best about them: inarguable reflections of their greatness in moments throughout the day. The portfolio once filled with evidence of mistakes and misbehaviors becomes filled with inner wealth.

My intention is to hijack children into a new portfolio where they see themselves as people of great value; to play hardball through great creative larceny, where we make success impossible to avoid.

Shamu's Great Trick

If you've ever seen Shamu the performing whale soar over a rope stretched across his pool, you might have wondered how a four-ton marine mammal is taught to perform this trick.

Do the trainers hold a rope 20 feet in the air and wait for the behemoth to leap over it before giving him a reward? No. Do they hold it at the water's surface? No. They don't hold it just below the water's surface, either. They actually start the training process by putting the rope across the very bottom of the pool.

As soon as Shamu cruises over the rope the very first time, he is congratulated and gets a reward. The connection is quickly made: when I swim over the twisty thing, I get a treat and energetic praise. Once the trainers see that he figures that out, the rope is gradually moved upward until it's way up out of the water, at the apex of Shamu's jumping ability.

Shamu can't help but swim over the rope and reap his reward. In the Nurtured Heart Approach, we create the same level of inevitability. We find ways to energize what the child is doing right even when nothing seems to be happening ("Isaac, I see you're sitting quietly in your seat, really focused on your work!"); or even when things seem to be going south but he's not yet crossed the line ("Kevin, I see you're having strong emotions right now because Amy took your lunch box without asking first…but you aren't trying to grab it back out of her hands. Awesome self-control."). If Kevin hasn't broken a rule, there's success in the air—even if his temper is nearly boiling over and even if he may break a rule in the next instant. The truth is that, in this instant, *he hasn't.*

Waiting to catch a child being good is like laying the rope across the surface of the water: Shamu *might* get over it at some point, but only maybe, and only if you wait long enough. **To create success where it isn't already obvious, remember the beauty of lowering the rope and how that serves to solidly gain the greatness that everyone *really* wants.**

A child who is repeatedly hijacked into success and then recognized for it will come to feel a growing self-appreciation and sense of greatness. Inner wealth takes hold. An overall sense of being a great person deepens and internalizes. The child comes to live out of her greatness and inner wealth. Achievement and mastery blossom from this new portfolio of greatness. She'll do it all in her own way, of her own volition, and from her own internal sense of who she is and who she wants to be in this world.

A child who is acting out is going to take a break from this behavior at some point, even if she's having the worst day of her life. At that moment, "pause the footage" and purposefully create a moment of success:

"Lana, I notice that you are not calling names or pushing others out of the way while waiting in line to get supplies. That's real patience, thoughtfulness and cooperation."

"Jesse, I appreciate the decision you made to ignore the interruption. That was a great choice and great judgment."

"Julio, your intuition is very innovative and it has inspired several of your

Notch it Up: *When You Encounter a Really Tough Kid*

The classic approach to dealing with the toughest children is to keep ramping up consequences in response to repeat or escalating offenses. This is a trap. The challenging child is running the show, and he knows it. Ramping up conventional consequences brings heightened reactive emotion and energized relationship. This relationship is clearly discernable to the child, and he ends up construing ever-escalating consequences as rewards (inadvertent $100 bills). Anyone who has been in the position of having to come up with yet another more severe consequence to try to rein in a difficult child knows that this tactic ultimately leaves you feeling helpless.

When I work with gang kids who have their game faces on, I take positivity to a really high level of ferocity. I operate under the assumption that this kid's life depends on me winning at this juncture in the path. When I take these recognitions and appreciations to whatever level is necessary to break through to his greatness, I know I've won (and so has the kid). I drop the rope to the bottom of the pool. If that doesn't work, I am relentless in laying down a whole web of rope. Lo and behold, at some level, I find a way to get to the kid's greatness every time.

These moments where the adult is most challenged are the pivotal moments. The only way to get through to a really challenging child is to dig in and ramp up the level of energy to what's needed. This, coupled with a refusal to give energy to negativity, has made the difference every time in my many years of work with the most difficult children around.

In the moment where the child is going to the mat to rope you into energizing his negative behaviors, it's easy to fall into the trap of reactively spewing out consequences in an effort to gain power. When you catch yourself sliding into your own negative place while facing off with an exquisitely difficult child, try *resetting yourself* to finding greatness. Take all the strength and power of negative emotions—worries, fears, doubts—and channel that energy into furthering your commitment to relentlessly energize the positive. Try your best to remember, in those moments, that the lion's share of your transformative power is in stretching your expressions of recognition and appreciation, from your heart and soul. You'll only need to trust me on this point until you have that breakthrough experience yourself...with that kid in your classroom whom everyone else thought was a lost cause.

Seek out levels of success and appreciation beyond any level you have previously encountered. There is always more breadth, depth and height to be explored in the adventure of reaching a child. In my experience, as soon as that level is found—even if it's 14 levels beyond anything I needed to reach any other challenging child—*the child will respond.*

Whatever the child is doing to try to get you to lose hold of your refusal to energize negative behaviors, make a conscious choice to *not* give it any energy in that moment. If you know you are going to need to 'freak out' at some point, resolve to do it privately. The child has zero access to that button; he'll never even know it existed. Then, recommit to finding yet more ways to reflect positivity—to find real evidence of success and hold it up to the light of day. In my own experience, more positivity is always the way through these situations.

All of this is not about fixing the child in front of me; it's about controlling the way I show up in this situation. And using the approach gets smoother and simpler and more effective with each such challenge.

classmates to trust their intuition as well. It is great that you can listen to what you feel inside and use it to be creative."

"Rachel, you are staying in your seat instead of getting up and walking around the room. Thanks so much for following our rule about that; it makes the lesson go smoothly. You're choosing to not get distracted or distract others and you're really contributing to the focused atmosphere of the room."

You can also lower the rope in more subtle ways when rules aren't being broken. For example: If a child can't seem to get homework right but does hand it in completed on the day it's due, you might say, "Travis, you always get that homework in on time. Very responsible." If Travis hands in the homework a day late, lower the rope a little more: "Travis, I know it's hard to come to me and hand me the homework packet a day late. You're risking disapproval from me in order to follow up on your commitment. That's courageous." Don't tell Travis, "Now if you could only apply yourself a little more and get more of your work right," or "Maybe next time you'll get your work handed in on time." Language like this raises the rope too high and violates your intention to adhere to Stands 1 and 2 of the approach. Have faith that, as his inner wealth continues to accrue as a result of the foundation you are building, Travis will come to fulfill his commitments fully, despite any previous patterns or complicating situations at home. I have seen this over and over: once a child comes to internalize these reflections of greatness and success, he inevitably begins to act out greatness at ever-escalating levels.

When you nourish a child with an Experiential Recognition, let the child bask in that moment of being energized with no undercurrent of negativity. Remember: even pep talks ("Travis, I just *know* you'll get that homework done on time next time!") subtly energize the negative. Let the child clear the rope and fully digest his new or renewed connection before raising that rope any higher. You will sense when that can be done; your students will signal you when they are ready for greater challenges.

By holding the intention to put the rope wherever necessary to let the child clear it—and, in clearing it, receive abundant energy from us, his 'guides' in this adventure of life—we commit to creating success for the child no matter what. *We refuse to forget to energize success.* This may involve lowering the rope of expectation all the way to the bottom of the pool, but in time, the child will come to accept that he'll get connected with you in a success-oriented way (but *not* for breaking rules) when he swims over it. Resolve that this is not going to be a fair contest: that you *will* "win" the child into success; you *will* reflect his greatness; and you'll do so with intensity. Remain steadfast as you continually see and acknowledge the child's every increment in the direction of success.

Confront Students...with Appreciation

Expect and assume the child's competency in each moment, but create a situation where this competency is guaranteed. Instead of negativity-energizing confrontations (lectures, pleading, nagging, bargaining, yelling), confront your students with their intrinsic greatness and with appreciation of the ways in which that greatness is expressed. This will give you a transformed sense of how powerful positive confrontations can be.

Certainly, not every child is going to get great grades or excel in every subject. Not every child can be popular or beautiful or good at sports. Some kids struggle with learning disabilities or symptoms that might have earned them an ADHD diagnosis. Despite genetic and biochemical factors, my experience has shown me that the brain's wiring can be altered with the right kind of intervention, and neuroscience now confirms that weak brain pathways can be strengthened and new and stronger pathways can be formed. Each child's unique strengths can be honed and drawn out through focused positivity.

These two techniques—Active Recognition and Experiential Recognition—provide sturdy foundations for creating an environment of positivity in the classroom. The next two techniques build on these foundations to expand opportunities to see, acknowledge and foster greatness in each of your students.

Notching it Up!
Add Heart to Your Recognitions

To some readers, this notion of pouring on recognitions and appreciations may seem, at first, a bit over the top—a false way of spinning the reality of situations. Consider this: whether we say something negative, say something positive or say nothing at all, *we are creating spin.* We are choosing what we observe and how we comment upon it. There are levels upon levels of gratitude to be stumbled upon, and you can choose to go there. This isn't false, it's just a shift in perspective.

There's no need to gush or cheerlead (actually undesirable in this approach). On the contrary: we are accessing a pure and totally authentic form of recognition. Imagine that your vocal cords have a direct connection to your most loving, heartfelt self. **Keep it honest and speak from your heart.**

Positive recognitions can be spoken purely from the mind, with stunning effect. However, after watching thousands of educators and the responses of the children with whom they are communicating, it's clear that when one adds *heart* to the equation, the words have more impact. Try notching this technique up—accelerating its power—by speaking from and staying in your heart. If you find yourself moving out of that space, you can choose to reset yourself back into it.

Tina is a parent who found exactly what she needed in this concept of notching it up through the heart. Her son, Andrew, is a highly intelligent and intense child who had been very resistant to his mother's attempts to point out his greatness. After reading this book, she began to implement the notching-up strategies. Here is how she described what transpired:

> We had an hour-long conversation about values and how to conduct one's self in different situations. It was so awesome…HE led the conversation, he voiced his values and truths. I went deep inside myself and concentrated on the energy emanating from my heart. I got into my heart with intention, and everything I said to honor him came directly, with almost physical energy, from my heart!
>
> "Andrew, you are talking to me in a calm voice about something you feel very passionate about. You are showing tremendous calm."
>
> "Andrew, I am so moved by your presence of mind and your self-awareness. You are communicating to me about what you

believe to be desirable behavior. Your ability to determine what is important takes so much maturity and thoughtfulness...I am in awe of you and your self-awareness."

"Andrew, the fact that your own internal compass guides your behavior indicates to me your strong sense of right and wrong."

"Your sense of calm and openness right now show me your integrity and independent thinking."

"Andrew, you are being so honest with me and yourself right now. You are being true to yourself."

If I hadn't thought to notch it up from that heart place, I might not have had the ability to appreciate him for going there. As it was, I went on and on like this the entire day. I could not get over this amazing internal guidance I was seeing Andrew manifest...how openly he was sharing with me about his own values, his own moral code. It really blew me away. Then, a couple days later, I asked him whether he remembered what I said to him in that conversation. He said, "That I'm mature and have self-awareness."

Since this beautiful time together, it feels like he trusts me to nurture him. He has been calmer. That special time I spent with my son will always be in my heart!

Try this experiment to get a feel for what it means to speak from the heart. This practice comes from Heart Rhythm Meditation, which was developed by Puran and Susanna Bair based on ancient meditation practices. Regular practice of this form of meditation promotes greater sensitivity, compassion, appreciation and joy—the ability to "live from the heart."

Sit tall on a chair or cushion, with your spine erect. Let your hands relax on your legs. Close your eyes and begin to take long, steady breaths, without forcing. Exhale deeply to make room for the next inhalation, keeping the transition between inhalation and exhalation as noiseless as possible.

Then, locate your heartbeat with the pulse point on one wrist or by putting one hand to your chest. Inhale smoothly for eight beats, then exhale smoothly for eight beats. Spend at least five minutes with this breath pattern. When you're done, open your eyes and sense your mood and level of appreciation. Feel the awareness of the heart center. From this place, from-the-heart conveyances arise with ease. This practice, over time, confers the ability to access this great inner realm whenever it feels called for.

When Cooley Middle School psychologist Mary Martin taught a severely anxious student how to do this simple breathing meditation, his ability to control his anxiety was vastly improved. Whenever he saw Mary, he would put his hand to his pulse point and say "Got it." (See Resources section for more about Heart Rhythm Meditation.)

Recognition from the heart tends to be effortlessly rich, textured and varied. In contrast, when teachers stay in their heads, so to speak, grasping for words and trying laboriously to string them together in the best possible way, they tend to struggle more to remember what to say.

Use the linguistic ideas supplied in the previous chapter (Values and Qualities Worth Acknowledging) to support you in growing the breadth and width of this language so that it can eventually flow easily from your heart. At first, you may want to try creating Experiential Recognitions from your head, using the values presented in that list just to get the hang of it. You may eventually find, however, that comments sourced from the logical mind often run thin and dry—or may even run out. With heart-centered recognitions, you'll find you won't even need that list of values because you'll have your own 'online resource center' right in the center of your body. You'll come to trust that, in the moment, your heart will have exactly the right words.

Any time you need guidance from within, give your heart a voice. Give it ten votes. Give it ten *thousand* votes.

Chapter 5

Celebrating Rules Not Broken and Requests Honored: Proactive and Creative Recognitions

ONE MOTHER I SAW AS A CLIENT was truly "fried" (her own descriptor) from her efforts to control her teenage daughter. The girl reportedly argued and swore constantly. A slew of meds and several psychiatric hospitalizations had not helped. In our very first meeting, this mom was in my office lamenting when I urged her to simply tell her daughter her heart's truth of this very moment, which was that the girl looked angry but was neither cussing nor arguing.

The mother believed that applauding the absence of undesirable behaviors would inspire those exact behaviors. I acknowledged that her fear was understandable but convinced her to try anyhow. She followed my advice and found a way to express honest appreciation for the truth of the moment.

Her daughter hesitated a few seconds in receipt of this recognition, then lit up, smiled and thanked her mother for appreciating her. The mother lit up, too, and smiled back. From there, the new and much-improved flow of connection began to roll out. I made a point of 'confronting' this mother for the incredibly great recognition she gave her daughter despite being "fried." I had witnessed the start of this mom's journey from ordinary and conventional parenting to extraordinary parenting. Her daughter, in turn, moved into a new realm of extraordinariness as well; her immense intensity became a gift to herself and the world around her.

Imagine yourself standing in front of your class. Everyone's quiet and attentive; no one's breaking any rules. Could one or more of your students be yelling out at this moment, disturbing the class with unacceptable sounds or words or distracting other students with name-calling or taunts? Yes, but they're not. They aren't throwing things at each other or getting up and running around the room. No one is engaging in any acts of aggression. They know how to do all of those things, right? If they were to choose to engage in those behaviors, there's little you could do to stop them.

Here's the truth: children really are free to break rules. When they're not, they are *choosing* not to, and this gives you virtually unlimited options for positive reflection. **As long as a child isn't breaking a rule, you can shine a light on the greatness he's displaying in making that choice.**

Yes, when children behave well, they're just doing what's expected, what's correct and moral and right. But we all have been around kids when they are being oblivious to the rules and creating a disruption. We all, therefore, know how wonderful it is when rules aren't being broken and how grateful we are for this choice. Proactive Recognition is a way to activate and share that gratitude.

I grew up in New York City and worked my way through school driving a taxi on weekends. Because of the intimacy I developed with the city—which included watching the World Trade Center being built—I can say that every single moment when planes are *not* flying into buildings is a miraculous one. I don't have to wait until Thanksgiving to feel my gratefulness. I can feel gratitude any time I desire—and, it turns out, gratitude has level upon level of depth and breadth to which I was not exposed as a child. Every time I stumble upon or invoke a new level, a more expansive level of appreciative living is revealed.

Consider my work with recidivist fire setters. These kids had been through court programs where they were made to watch video of burn victims. They certainly had heard their fair share of "Don't you ever do that again." And they had gone on to set more fires.

I told them the truth of how grateful I was that they had not thus far set a fire on this particular day. When I implored parents and other important adults to do the same for these kids, it often set off a core fear that I've seen again and again: "But they'll set a fire if I say that!" They realized the fear was unfounded after they took the leap, made this brash appreciation and saw the outcome. Once these children were experiencing the energy they needed in the form of gratitude-laden relationship, they no longer needed to seek the convoluted version of connection and relationship they had once obtained by setting fires.

Third Technique: Proactive Recognition

Most teachers and parents give lots of energized connection when rules are broken. With Proactive Recognition, we turn the energetic equation right-side-up by **expressing genuine gratitude when the child does not break rules.** This offers many opportunities to recognize self-control and healthy expressions of power.

Proactive Recognition clarifies limits in a new way—when the child is *in-bounds*, not when he's out-of-bounds. We might appreciate a child for choosing not to be aggressive when frustrated or angered; express gratitude to a class for handling a delay in the lesson plan well; or recognize a child for not interrupting a class experiment.

We live in a society that unhesitatingly acts when a rule is broken. Even when a rule seems about to be broken, we are so energetically *there,* so alive and present and responsive. This is society's default. With Proactive Recognition, we go to 'system preferences' and change that setting to be 'in gear' and excited when rules are *not* broken.

If Amelia is sitting in your classroom and gazing out the window, consider all she is *not* doing that she *could* be doing.

"Amelia, I see you are not speaking out of turn. Thanks for being respectful of others' need to share."

"Amelia, you are not getting out of your seat during study time. You're setting a great example of being cooperative and present."

"Amelia, you aren't distracting yourself with doodling or fiddling with your mechanical pencil. You look like you're really listening to the lesson."

Amelia is not distracting anyone, copying another student's paper or back-talking. Choosing to acknowledge her for those choices moves you into that realm of extraordinary relationship—the kind that informs a child, in the moment, that she is truly valued and honored and gets that connected energy and presence from you in response to that choice to follow the rules.

It may seem absurd to offer recognition to a child for *not* breaking a rule, but consider this: Do you know a child who is aggressive? Who likes to curse? Who frequently disrupts the classroom? How does that feel? Take a moment and allow yourself to feel that feeling, which may be quite familiar to you if you've been a teacher or a parent for any length of time. Do you feel excited when the disruptive, cursing or aggressive child does *not* do his or her usual stunts in the classroom? Are you grateful? This feeling of authentic appreciation is what makes Proactive Recognitions feel like the real and honest truth.

This technique is pure gold for the child who is hungry for recognition and who likes to pretend that he doesn't know the rules (although he does). With this technique, we're able to accomplish two important ends:

1. We can teach rules not by energizing children for approaching the line, threatening to cross the line or crossing it, but by standing with them on the positive side of that imaginary line. The message is, "Hey, wow, look how you're solidly on the positive side of this line!" and perhaps reflecting a value or two being embodied through that choice.

2. We make success impossible to avoid because no child can break all of the rules all of the time. No child can break rules 24/7, though many are thusly accused.

For the challenging child, rule-breaking is the most predictable, reliable way to get energized involvement in an instant, even if the adult is busy or distracted. Rule-breaking guarantees energetic intimacy—not congruent connectivity, but a dose of *perceived,* non-nourishing intimacy. We want to connect when the rules are not being threatened or broken, and we want to give credit to the child for that choice. They certainly get 'credit' for making a choice when they *do* break the rules. Why not give credit when they don't?

A Warning against Warnings

The teacher who warns a child against misbehavior that has not yet happened is offering up evidence that she is not in the moment, but rather that she is fearfully anticipating the future. This only contributes to the child's existing portfolio of feeling celebrated for her poor choices.

Warnings give energy and relationship for acting-out or anticipated acting-out. The child 'reads' this as a lack of faith in her ability to use healthy power and control. A meta-message of fear on the part of the teacher underlies the warning.

We'll take a closer look at warnings and other accidental ways of energizing negativity when applying a consequence in the next chapter.

State Rules in the Negative

It's hard to enforce a limit that hasn't been set. A referee can't easily call an infraction for stepping on an out-of-bounds line if the line is blurry, broken or non-existent.

Proactive Recognition requires that you, the educator, be completely clear and precise about the rules of your classroom. **The clarity required here is best served by stating rules in the *negative*.** This means that instead of the standard 'positive' rules (be kind, be respectful, keep your hands to yourself and so on), your classroom rules will be negative versions (no hitting, no name-calling, no raising your voice at others, no pushing and so on). This may run counter to everything you've been taught or experienced until now.

For most of my early years as a family therapist, positively-stated rules seemed not only natural but correct. As I worked more and more with challenging children, however, I came to see that rules stated in the positive are counterproductive. It's like playing basketball on a court with wavy, fuzzy lines as a boundary rather than straight, solid lines. As long as players stay near the center, all is fine, but as soon as anyone approaches that boundary, chaos arises. What's in? What's out? Where's the boundary here? To teach rules, you need to clarify rules, and the clearest way to state them is in the negative: in other words, by spelling out what is *not* the desirable behavior. Everything that *is* desirable behavior is then fair game for positive recognition.

Consider that rules stated in the typical positive way are just begging to be tested. What, exactly, does it mean to follow the rule "be respectful?" How do students know where the line is between respectful and disrespectful? In most classrooms, children are quickly dressed down for being *disrespectful*—but do they really know where the line is between that forbidden place and the range of *experiences* of being respectful? Do we really know exactly and precisely where that line is for us? Does it move back and forth depending on our mood or shifts in our sense of right and wrong? With that fuzzy line, challenging kids can play on the boundary and get abundant relationship. Meanwhile, the good kids get annoyed and the marginal kids take notes.

The fact is that children hear rules in the negative anyway. When I ask children what the rules are, they almost always state them in the negative, even if their classroom has positive rules. This may be reflective of how they hear and digest them, and it provides confirmation that children crave the level of clarity offered by negative rules.

Rules are not about what a child *should* do, they are about what a child should *not* do. Couching rules in negative language gives adults so much more to work with when offering specific positive reflections for rules not being broken. Although you *can* use this approach with positive rules, they make things more complicated and less pixelated.

When I first experimented with the linguistic strangeness of complimenting children for rules not broken, I was stunned by the powerful impact of confronting children with success around the rules. They *got it* so quickly, and before long, *I knew that they knew the new rules, and they knew that I knew.* Enforcing the rules in their new version became infinitely simpler, and negatively stated rules made it infinitely easier to detect when rules were *not* being broken. As in sports, either your foot is on or over the line, or it's in-bounds.

I found that these kids loved the clarity of "No teasing (or disrespect or name-calling)" and they loved being recognized for making the choice not to break rules. They had previously been exposed to constant admonitions and pressures of "no this or that," but they had never before felt the heartwarming pleasure of being appreciated for rules not broken.

Before starting to use Proactive Recognitions, take some time to review and re-word your classroom rules so that they fit into this negative format. Here are a few examples to get you started:

No hitting	No name-calling
No disrespect	No bad manners
No irresponsibility	No breaking things
No arguing	No threats
No teasing	No tantrums

Discuss the new rules with your class if you like, but you don't have to. Simply begin to apply the technique of Proactive Recognition and you'll see how effective this makes you at conveying the very rule-based lessons you have always desired to teach. Students will quickly download these newly worded rules as they are energized for following them.

Here's another story from early childhood educator Pat Bethke. It's a great example of the use of Proactive Recognition in a situation where a child is successfully coping with strong emotions; it also portrays how the various techniques of the approach work seamlessly with one another:

> *Chen had limited verbal skills because he came from a non-English-speaking family. He and his classmates were in our school's 'dramatic play center,' which currently was serving as a grocery store. One little girl was ringing up groceries at the cash register. Chen was standing next to her with his hands on his hips and a pouty, angry expression on his face. I walked over and described what I saw. To the child at the register I said, "It looks like you are buying groceries and ringing them up on the cash register. Chen is here, and he looks like he is waiting to use the cash register, too." Then I said: "I can see that your face is a little angry, Chen. Even so, you are not grabbing the cash register away, you are not yelling and you are waiting patiently. I like that you are handling those strong feelings." Chen immediately stomped away and sat down, elbows on the table, chin in his hands and the biggest drooping lower lip I had seen in a long time. I walked over to him and again told him how well he was handling his frustration with not being able to use the cash register. I acknowledged the great choice he made in coming over and taking his own break. I told him that I trusted that, when he was done, he would rejoin us. When he did, I gave him more recognitions and acknowledged how great it was that he was engaging with us again and had found something else to do.*

Having reconfigured your classroom rules and become adept at handing out Proactive Recognitions, what do you do, then, when the rules are broken? Consistently, calmly and with as little energy as possible, enact a consequence in the form of time-out/reset.

When a Rule Is Broken

Rule-breaking is generally seen as something to be avoided. In this approach, however, we send a message to students that **at every moment, they have a choice. They don't have to be perfect. No one does. They can break the rules any time they want.** We couldn't stop them even if we wanted to; it has always been their choice. As much as we'd like to keep this a secret, every child knows this all too well.

Keeping this truth in mind allows us to honor children, with heartfelt honesty, for all their choices to not break rules. When rules do get broken, a truly un-energized consequence (the reset) works with Proactive Recognitions and other recognitions to move a child to *not want to break rules*.

Chapter 6 addresses the reset in detail, including suggestions about how to introduce it to your class, but this should be enough to get you started: Say the student's name, then say "reset." As soon as the rule-breaking stops, give appreciation for a reset well done, for rules now being followed, and for positive values and qualities being demonstrated by this choice.

Ongoing acknowledgments of rules not broken and consistent, un-energized enforcement when rules *are* broken work as counter-balancing forces to hold students firmly and securely in time-in. **As you demonstrate that rule-breaking and boundary-pushing are no longer effective ways to create energized relationship with you, breaking rules and pushing boundaries become just plain boring!**

Rule-breaking is most often not a mistake; it is almost always a choice. Following the rules is a choice, too, and a when a child makes it, he is being wise and skillful. When he has the impulse to break a rule and doesn't, he is using great control and healthy power. This perspective gives you even more fodder for reflecting success.

If the unspoken agreement around rules between you and students were spoken aloud, it might go something like this: "I appreciate your choice when you decide not to break the rules. I also know that, at any time, you can choose to break them. When you do so, you get a consequence, but I don't take it personally.

"You get none of ME when you make that choice. My being is detached for those moments, and I'll reset to honoring you when you are back to not breaking the rules. As soon as you finish that consequence, you're back in the game. I recognize that rule-breaking is a natural part of your exploration, but I sure

Notch it Up: *A New Take on Critical Thinking*

Most educators have heard at some point that, for every criticism doled out to a child, one should give a certain number of positive statements. The popular PBIS (Positive Behavioral Intervention and Support) program advocates a 4:1 ratio of praise to criticism; DrSpock.com recommends a more generous 10:1 ratio; and other approaches cover pretty much every ratio in between. I personally believe the appropriate ratio is infinity:0.

Most of us have great critical thinking skills, having had these honed through years of education and interaction in the world at large. But critical thinking also makes a wonderful tool for providing children with critical analysis of their *greatness*.

Once the intention is set to direct our critical faculties into this endeavor, we can use those skills to uncover level upon level of greatness. All the lessons we were dying to teach get planted and nurtured in sweeter ways through recognition. Calling out what's wrong becomes unnecessary: those weeds diminish on their own for lack of energetic 'water.'

do appreciate when you make the great decision to *not* break rules. When you make that decision, you get all the credit."

To the best of your ability, remain emotionally detached when students break rules, especially now that you know that acting out is really just an unconscious ploy to try to get connected with the gift of YOU. Having this insight gives you the power to reset them to greatness.

Rules Become a Path to Greatness

If asked, students almost always say they don't like rules—mainly because they only hear about the rules when they're breaking them and getting the resultant lecture or punitive consequence! All of this slides into the child's portfolio *as failure, failure, failure*. But when you start using Proactive Recognition, something amazing happens: children start to *like* rules. They come to see rules as a way to success. Eventually, the more rules you create, the happier your students will be, because they'll have even more opportunities to be recognized for rules not broken. Rules become ways for children to appreciate themselves and others—a new source of fuel for their inner wealth and greatness.

Create a broad range of rules that reflect your students as whole people. Tell the truth of this moment; leave the past and future out. Even if a child has just finished breaking five rules simultaneously and has served the consequence of his reset, see the next moment when he's not breaking any rules as an opportunity to celebrate!

Doesn't thanking a child for not hitting give her the idea and inspiration to do just that? *Only if you are still engaging in some traditional form of upside-down response to negativity.* If you have not established a solid time-in, a child may still believe she's going to get more out of you by choosing to break a rule. In that case, thanking her for not hitting might encourage her to try clobbering her friend to see whether the juice still flows from that source. If Proactive Recognitions have this effect, check that you're holding to the first Stand (no energy to negativity) and offering ample Active and Experiential Recognitions (relentlessly energizing the positive) per the second Stand. Notch it up until you find a new level where it hits home.

Fourth Technique: Creative Recognition

Kind and loving teachers tend to make requests to students using impeccably polite wording. *Please do your assignment without talking to your neighbor. Would you please pick up your trash? Will you close your books and put them away, please?* In the process, they are accidentally conveying that students have a choice. And for the energy-challenged child, such politely worded requests advertise that refusal is a quick way to lure the teacher into the energy-for-negativity dance. If the child holds out long enough, she can get more relationship with everyone in the room and maybe even with the principal or the school counselor—simply by refusing to comply with a request made by an adult. She doesn't do it consciously; she just wants the intimacy and connection. Creative Recognition defines a method for making requests in a new way—one that makes compliance virtually unavoidable, then holds the child in esteem for all the qualities of greatness expressed in his compliance.

This is a technique to really amp up for the especially challenging child—the one who seems wholly unwilling to let go of his addiction to getting energized for bad behavior. Consider a child like this a great blessing: he's going to push you to levels of creativity and intensity that will benefit every child in your classroom. You are going to become a hijacker; you're going to commit perfect larceny; you're going to *ignite* greatness in even the most resistant child! (Recently, a new acquaintance asked me what I do for a living. Before I thought much about my answer, I blurted, "I'm an arsonist!" Then I explained that what I ignite is *greatness.*)

Every day, children are expected to do certain things without being told or in response to a pleasant request from an adult. Once they reach school age, for example, they're supposed to handle the basics of self-care and grooming. They're expected to get themselves dressed, go to school, and behave themselves reasonably well across a variety of situations; perhaps they're expected to do certain chores around the house or in the classroom. Average children can manage all of this fairly well, complying with expectations without being asked or with a gentle reminder. Intense children, however, will refuse to do even these basic things. They have learned, through experience, that refusing to do what's asked or expected is a consistently great way to extract energy, connection and relationship: it produces the most entertaining and animated responses from their favorite toys. The portfolios of most such children are full of evidence that, when they comply with expectations, life gets boring (at most, earning them a low-key "thank you" or "good job") and they feel relatively invisible. When they resist, refuse or hold out long enough, the fireworks begin.

With Creative Recognition, we essentially *create compliance before the child can refuse to comply.* We then give the child all the credit, with plenty of energy, presence and connection in return for the successful choice. Over time, this can fill even the most recalcitrant child's portfolio with evidence that *he is* responsive and that *he will* get energetically nurtured when he follows the rules and complies with requests. It's the beginning of the end of the child's addiction to negativity.

One particular child, Joseph, got sent to the principal's office almost every day (except for the days on which there were field trips or parties!). The first reward he'd get for refusing to comply with requests from his teacher was lots of energized connection with everyone in the classroom. Once sent out, he got to dance down the hallway with a human being, extracting even more connection. If he was especially needy that day, he'd greet the principal by flinging himself on the floor like a jellyfish. Although he seemed to be suffering, what was going on energetically for Joseph was: *I've hit the jackpot!* The energy dished out in response to Joseph's adversarial behavior translated, to him, into being treated like royalty. He had all the administrators and office assistants falling all over themselves in their attempts to right the ship.

I was asked to work with the parents, who described Joseph as extremely oppositional at home. I taught them about Creative Recognition via the Shamu story. "Put rope all over the place at the bottom of the tank," I told them. "Be tricky. Make it foolproof. Get him to be cooperative without his realizing it, then applaud him for it."

Rolling his eyes, Dad responded, "You don't know Joseph." Several days later the dad called me with this story: He was picking his son up after school. As Joseph was climbing into the car and had the door almost shut, Dad said, "I need you to close the door" (an act that Joseph was almost in the throes of doing anyway). Dad followed this with thanks and recognition for Joseph complying with the request. I applauded Dad: "That's a home run." His story continued: seconds later, *after* Joseph had clicked on his seatbelt, Dad told him, "Joseph, put on your seatbelt." More relationship and recognition for Joseph following directions came on the heels of this second request. "That's a grand slam home run! That one was already in the bank," I told him. The father had created a sequence that created the successes and then produced a resounding buzz about it. This was a brilliantly executed series of Creative Recognitions!

It was only a matter of weeks before Joseph was highly cooperative. You could ask him the unthinkable—"Joseph, go do your homework" or "I need you to clean your room now"—and he would do so, cooperatively and well. He could easily clear that rope held at 25 feet, but only because his parents were willing to start with the rope as low as it could go.

"Could you," "Can you," "Please" or other such wobbly launches infer that the request is an option. Even worse, for the challenging student, it implies that by *not* complying with the request, he will get what he always has: juicy connectivity. With this technique, any time you make a request, be careful not to form it into a question. Clearly state what you want. Save the energy that once went into constructing a polite request; put it instead into appreciation of the student who has complied. Real-time recognition is more nourishing to the child than habitual politeness.

Compliance to such requests and your response to that compliance serve as stepping-stones to greater requests. You are bringing that rope down far enough to give the child the pleasurable, nutritious experience of being recognized and appreciated for doing something positive. This experience gives birth to intrinsic motivation: the beginnings of an internal desire to do what is needed in a collaborative and cooperative way. Make failure impossible.

"I need you to push in your chair."

"Help open the blinds...pull the slider to the left."

"Go ahead and take out your homework."

"I want you to pack up your things."

Let's say you see Shane, a difficult student, getting ready to hand in a class project. You say, "Shane, I need you to pass your project toward the front." You immediately honor his choice to follow your directions: "Thanks so much for listening to my request and following my directions. Your cooperation is so appreciated. Great choice, Shane."

Try making a request so simple that it goes under the radar of defiance. "Tricia, hold this dry marker for a second," at which point you hand it to her, do something for a second or two, then purposefully turn back to her and appreciate her cooperative choice. "I really appreciate that you cooperated when I asked. Thanks so much for helping out."

When the difficult child is on her way through the door of the classroom, tell her, "I need you to go into the classroom right now." Unless she balks and backs out of the doorway, you've *created* a moment of success. Jump on it. "You heard my request to go into class, and it was like you read my mind. You were there in the blink of an eye. Thanks for being so attentive." You undoubtedly know what it feels like when a child doesn't cooperate; let the memory of this—be it frustration, anger or other similar feelings—motivate you to authentic, heart-centered appreciation. Avoid any tinge of sarcastic addendum that might be tempting if this child has been hard to manage in the past.

With Creative Recognition, we can also get creative in terms of energizing every movement in a positive direction. Even if the child doesn't comply fully or instantly, you can still energize him for *any movement in the direction of compliance.* This reflects the notion of lowering the rope until the child clears it and gets energetically fed in this new, congruent manner.

Let's say you tell Charlie to sit down in his chair. He doesn't go right away, but he is already facing it. "Charlie, you're listening and cooperating by heading toward your chair." Then, if he takes a step toward it, you can energize that. Draw him into success by energizing each increment toward it. Make miracles from molecules; pixelate as much as necessary. Break down students' actions and choices far enough, and you *will* find something to celebrate. The more challenging the child, the more necessary it will be to use these small, simple movements to start the momentum going. You will see a big impact in a difficult child as the shift to cooperation takes hold.

You can use this technique for emotions, too. Co-author Melissa's son Noah once began to have a tantrum when she reset him and then requested that he leave with her from a concert that was in progress. Noah cried loudly as they walked along the sidewalk. Melissa said, "I appreciate that even though you're really angry and upset, you're walking along with me instead of making me drag or carry you." Noah didn't exactly stop his hollering but took a momentary pause. "I was just about to ask you to calm down, and I didn't even have to. It was like you read my mind and knew what I wanted," she told him. "Great work at using your inner strength to calm down!" While answering "I can't calm down," Noah nonetheless calmed a little more. She jumped right in with a series of appreciations about his self-control and power. He calmed even more and tilted his tear-streaked face up to her. "Mommy, I DID it!" he said with pride. Tantrum diverted into a moment of total success, for which Noah got all the credit. No attempt was made to get Noah to squash his emotional response to the situation; this will help him maintain a healthy relationship with tough emotions.

What if a child refuses, in the end, to comply with your request? A consequence is called for. After the consequence is completed and you energize the child for serving that consequence, the request still holds. Repeat it if you like, but don't escalate or say anything about the past refusal. It's a new moment and a new opportunity.

Notch it Up *at the Soul Level*

Another way to get creative with your recognitions: recognize students for the way in which their core qualities have a positive impact. Peer into your own heart for qualities for which every human being has some capacity because they are part of the human condition: compassion, kindness, a loving nature, empathy, inner joy, generosity. Call students out for incontrovertible qualities they are expressing in the moment:

"Jesse's calmness really helps bring focus to the room."

"Having you in this class gives everyone a little extra energy boost, Stella. We love the enthusiasm!"

"Pablo, you're listening to me so well. I can see your compassion and kindness."

"You are sparking so much wisdom, Julio, by sharing your intelligent insights. Your contributions have everyone participating in this lively dialogue."

"Jason, thank you for handling your annoyance so well. It shows how much you care about justice and fairness."

"Wendy, I appreciate how you speak out about what's right from your point of view. You have the greatness of a strong heart and concern for humanity. That is wonderful power."

"Justin, I really enjoy that I can rely on you to show up alert and involved. You are being very present in tackling this class project step by step. You are being wonderfully sensitive to the needs of the class and the assignment."

"Jennifer, your willingness to cooperate so beautifully with our class schedule today shows me your loving nature."

"Isaac, I see that all your friends are so happy to see you. You must be a loyal and fun friend to all of them to bring such smiles to their faces."

This notching-up technique works especially well with the toughest kids. Soul-level acknowledgements go beneath their defenses. Think back to the exchanges between Tina and her son Andrew (described in Notching it Up: Add Heart to Your Recognitions). Through a spiritual energy shift, Tina found a way to directly communicate her profound heart energy in response to Andrew's true, pure inner self. In one interaction with her son, she came to see the glory of his true self instead of the difficult child he always seemed to be. And she was right there with heartfelt notched-up reflections to capture him in those moments and confirm his greatness.

There's no overt request here, but there is an *unstated* one: "Do something great, or be greatness in a way that is you." The students cannot *not* comply, because you are energizing them for being their great selves and doing what is expected of them. You're telling the truth of their wonderfulness in a given moment and leaving the past and future out of it. These kinds of reflections are particularly good right after a time-out/reset when the next moments rely on your creativity in generating a new, ever greater flow of success.

By giving students compliments that resonate at a "soul-ular" level, you interact in a dimension of vibration and awareness that uplifts a spiritual transformation in you and encourages the same in those around you. In the more than 15 years of my own exploration of this practice, I've found that there are always more levels of soul sharing to explore and enjoy.

An Approach for the Whole Child

Early on in this book, we made it clear that this is a *whole-classroom* approach—it works only when applied to everyone in the room, difficult or not. This is also a *whole-child* approach. It is not an approach to use to address specific problems for individual children.

When I was still seeing patients in private practice, one couple's son had been wetting his bed for some time. They had unsuccessfully tried all sorts of interventions: pads with alarms that signal when moisture hits them, medications, reward systems, consequences, making the child change his own wet sheets. In consulting with me, they likely expected a direct, focused and targeted new technique to solve this particular problem.

Imagine their surprise when I told them that I was 100 percent certain that I could help but that what I could offer would *not* focus on the issue of enuresis. We would not talk about this problem at all. I explained to them that their child had already put two and two together and concluded that he got far more 'benefit' from maintaining the problem; anything I did to bring additional attention and energy to it would simply add fuel to his existing energetic impression. Instead, the parents would learn the Nurtured Heart Approach and apply it with their child. "Once his portfolio of first-hand experiences of success begins to internalize and multiply, the last thing he'll want to do is pee in the wrong place at the wrong time!" I told them. The intervention was successful, as it had been in all the other children in my practice who had been bed wetters.

To try 'fixing' any specific problem gives it energy, and the child is likely to perpetuate it in order to maintain that flow of connection. Another common example is the child who tends to stray off purpose while working on school assignments. Energizing this child for the many possibilities of any degree of related greatness—including not getting distracted or distracting others, effort and thought to portions of the work, organizational skills, openness, intuition, making steps toward completion, and even intelligent guesses—will do much for the child's ability to improve academically and his self-discipline in doing class work.

As a child comes to experience the truth of his successfulness, he will figure out how to solve his own ongoing problem. By refusing to accidentally fuel the problem and by offering a new train of recognition and appreciation, you help the child develop inner resourcefulness that will make other solutions unnecessary. He will carve out his own perfect ways of moving forward! And then, in addition to the child no longer having this one problem, we have a child who has a new perspective about *who he really is*. We can sit back and enjoy the bounty of the child's inner wealth as it rolls out into the world.

As you work with students who have specific issues, it can be tempting to concentrate on those 'problem areas.' This comes through especially strongly in the context of our huge inclination to focus on learning deficiencies in an academically oriented world. **Instead, recognize and appreciate the many aspects and qualities of every child in a broader scope of life, reflecting each student as a whole, contributing, valuable, purposeful and meaningful human being.**

Notch it Up: *The Resistant Child*

With intense, oppositional kids, a strong guilt/punishment/shame mindset can be firmly entrenched in their portfolio. Their experience of energy for negativity has given them a world view that will take time to shift. Children with this kind of history may mightily resist your appreciation and recognition at first. They may even look at you funny and tell you to leave them alone...or worse.

When a child resists positive, affirming connection, I construe it as a sign that it has at least registered and that my foot is in the door. We need to take the approach up a notch or a few notches so that it not only will resonate more deeply, but will signal to the child that this new energetic connection is here to stay.

If you encounter such resistance, you could say, "I get from your response that you think my compliments are annoying and you want me to stop. I'm not sure that's possible. Something inside me has changed." Tell the child or the class that you have had an awakening and realized that you have been focusing on what they do wrong but now you are seeing all they do right. In declaring yourself, you are simultaneously rolling out even more Active Recognition.

When facing a resistant child, stay positive by remembering what you are up to here and now: you are encouraging children to embrace their own intensity and express it in positive ways. For difficult children, this is a profound healing. Contrary to what's been said about and to them for as long as they can remember, they will find that they can control themselves and their intensity.

Through repeated experiences of being held in esteem in real time, the child learns to be truly positive with *herself.* She no longer has to perpetuate the habit of spinning her wheels on inner dialogue surrounding problems, fears, doubts and worries. As you stick to your Stands and as this child grows in her greatness, she learns to stand in that greatness by making it an integral part of her endeavors, interests, purpose and vision of how to be in this world.

Even those who have never been considered difficult may find a compliment to be overwhelming. If the compliment has depth and meaning plus the power of experiential inference, and if a child has only had exposure to basic praise (like "thank you" and "good job"), then this new style might be hard to digest at first. Typical reactions might be to deflect or discount it, giggle nervously and shrug it off, change the subject, or dive into some sort of activity. The child is not allowing himself to appreciate the moment and to stand in his greatness.

You can create that moment for even the most difficult child by notching it up at these pivotal points instead of shrinking away from children who pose strong challenges. You are helping these children see that they can bypass their *own* initial inner resistance to appreciating themselves. As you model this, they will drink in this new energetic impression.

"But It Feels Silly to Make a Big Deal Over Little Successes."

I hear this fairly often, especially from people who consider themselves to be reserved and not prone to displays of enthusiasm. They try their best but can't seem to find the internal energy to make the language of the Nurtured Heart Approach carry an adequate energetic punch.

These individuals often have backgrounds in which they received little or no acknowledgement for successes aside from stratospheric ones—and sometimes not even for those. They did, however, often get abundantly energized for negativity, so they know first-hand what it's like to be around enthusiastic response to what's perceived as wrong by another. Coming from a background like this can make positivity feel like pulling teeth.

If this is to any extent a description of you or what you were exposed to growing up, consider this: The great news is that you know full well what it feels like to get fired up and make a fuss. Now simply make the fuss and get fired up about all that's good and great.

Take that same energy—really let yourself feel it as energy welling up in your body—and *direct it toward something positive.* Find one good thing and use that energy to propel yourself toward it, using the techniques described in this book.

Go ahead and wag your finger. Accuse, lecture or confront, but do it entirely on behalf of *greatness.* Do it with calm, steady, relentless energy. **Flipping the energy here is like flipping a magnet around so that it attracts instead of repels. Let the force be *with* you.**

"But the Real World Won't Be Like This…"

This is another common response from parents and educators who are in the early stages of exploring the Nurtured Heart Approach. They worry that the environment created by the approach in one place (the home or school) won't carry over to "real life" outside. People are going to be negative, even mean, and these adults fear that the child who comes to expect positivity will be confused, hurt, disappointed or unprepared when faced with the opposite.

It's true that we don't live in a Nurtured Heart world. But when a child gets attuned to a new default setting of appreciation, gratitude and greatness, he will naturally attract work and personal relationships that are supportive and nourishing. He will develop the ability to choose to not participate in relationships and situations that do not serve him and create new relationships and situations that do. The child who has had his own greatness nurtured develops the capacity to adapt brilliantly to life in ways that make it joyous and bring satisfaction. As you begin to 'be the approach' yourself, you'll see how this works in your own life.

A Quick Review of Techniques for Upholding Stand 2

Active Recognition
Seeing and acknowledging the details of moments lived, without judgment

Experiential Recognition
Teaching values by recognizing (and, when necessary, creating) moments of values lived and expressed and delivering them wrapped in appreciation

Proactive Recognition
Teaching rules by freely giving recognition of rules followed

Creative Recognition
Creatively bringing children the feeling of success for following directions or for expressing their intrinsic greatness

Combining the Approach with Academics

With all of this positive reflection and relationship and pumping-up of students' inner wealth, when, exactly, will you have time to teach? In reality, by applying this approach, you will actually end up accomplishing much *more* academically. You'll burn through more curriculum than you ever have before.

Let's break it down. Once you get beyond the initial learning curve, become facile with all four techniques, and learn to mix, match, and play with them in a way that suits you and your classroom, you can expect to spend about five to 10 seconds giving each recognition. It's not unreasonable to think of giving between 10 to 100 such recognitions a day, which amounts to no more than a few minutes of your class time. You may need a little more than this for a class that includes especially intense children.

The simplest, least time-consuming way to begin is by offering a strong, intense application of the approach (with more reflections of greatness and success) to all of your students. Broadcast recognitions loud and clear so that they impact everyone in the room. Recognize a whole row or table of students at a time if you see a way to give them a greatness recognition, but try to use student names when possible.

As soon as teachers try this approach in earnest, they see that it doesn't take up a lot of time and that the children's response makes the day go more smoothly. Most teachers find that the approach becomes seamlessly integrated with curriculum and that they accomplish much *more* work in a day as children accrue inner wealth and begin to feel recognized and appreciated in the ways described in these pages. Students become attuned to the needs of the classroom because they want to be there, want to participate, want to do their homework and want to be prepared.

Children who come to experience their greatness *act out* greatness, which carries over to the academic side of the equation. They become more present and open as learners and show up for class better prepared. They need less review and show more initiative. Many teachers report that they have to expand their curriculum because their students start to burn through it so quickly.

Create Opportunities for Students to Energize Each Other

In her seventh-grade advanced pre-algebra class at Cooley Middle School, Cari Prater had a great habit of following up after a student answered a question with an opportunity for the student's classmates to energize him or her. "How many of you appreciated the clarity of her answer?" she asked at one point, and several hands shot up. At times she gave the other students the opportunity to expand on the qualities they were identifying, and she elaborated when appropriate.

Cari also offered some charmingly original recognitions during the class: "Owen's bursting with inner joy!" "Look at Lydia's excited hand. Spirit fingers!" When some students didn't grasp the next step in the lesson, Cari labeled the looks on their faces not as confusion or difficulty, but as "silent intellectual protest." Great creativity!

"There are huge differences in my classroom since I started using the Nurtured Heart Approach," Cari told me after class. "My old 'MO' was yelling. My new one is recognizing kids who stay on task. When I started doing that, it was amazing how the rest quieted down."

Another teacher at Cooley, Celeste Elsey, had physically integrated the Nurtured Heart Approach into her special education classroom. On one wall, she had created the "Wall of Greatness" where, she told me, "The kids can hang anything they want, as long as it's positive—it can be schoolwork, artwork or anything that reflects their greatness. At first, they were too cool to put their schoolwork up, but once one kid started, everyone went with it. Now kids dig through their backpacks to find stuff to post."

She also created a 'Greatness Graffiti' area on a large tear-off pad. No inappropriate comments are allowed there, but when Celeste starts a new page with a reflection of greatness, the students eagerly add their own recognitions and enjoy reading what others have posted.

Tammy Jacobs, a therapist and Nurtured Heart Approach trainer in Mesa, Arizona, has figured out some brilliant ways to promote peer energizing in a 'boot camp' she does with tough kids ages 14 to 17 from all over the U.S., some of whom have gang affiliations. Here is her description:

In an aggression replacement class I taught, I used sheets of paper that only said "I am amazing" across the top. The ultimate purpose of these sheets is for these teens to accumulate stamps for every recognized success throughout the 10 weeks (they get really competitive over this), but I decided to do an activity with the almost-blank sheets first.

I asked two students to pass out the sheets and then asked for volunteers who would like to stand up and read their paper out loud. The first kid read quietly, "I am amazing." I thanked him and verbally reflected back what he'd said. Then another student stood up and read his paper, which of course said the same thing—"I am amazing"—but was read with a slightly different tone. Another eight or so continued to volunteer to stand and read the paper out loud. Finally, one student said, "They all say the same thing." I responded, "They do? I think they are all saying something different." I demonstrated what I meant by reading it with varying volumes and tones, some reflecting abundant self-worth, some reflecting more hesitancy.

Then I asked more students to raise their hand to read the phrase. They started to read it boastfully and loud, some with great inflection and with big smiles on their faces. When teachers walked through the room during class, I stopped them to read the phrase out loud. The kids really loved this.

After every student had read the paper, one asked the 'money question': "What makes me amazing?" I asked the rest of the class, "Who in here can tell Juan what makes him amazing? Use very specific details." I gave them some examples of what I meant: Having met him only that day, I could still point out how he was sitting in his seat, raising his hand to volunteer, and especially asking the 'money question!'

Almost half the kids raised their hands and began igniting Juan's greatness. They all rose to the occasion and amazed me! The look on Juan's face was indescribable.

Afterward, I asked him how he felt about all these things they are pointing out. "At first it felt really weird, but I really liked it." This set the stage for the rest of the class to be on fire (in a good way)!

In a subsequent class where there was lots of acting-out, I talked about how levels of the feel-good brain chemical serotonin increase when you give, receive and witness positive feedback. "What do you think might happen with negative feedback?" I asked them, and they all assumed that serotonin drops with put-downs and confrontations. I gave them recognition for this insightfulness, then redirected them to their experience a week earlier when we all read the handouts. I asked Juan if he remembered how it felt to be told all the ways in which he was amazing. "It felt good," he said, and all the other students said they liked it too. I asked them, "How about instead of having negative confrontations like the ones we had earlier in this class period, we pick someone each week to point out what makes him or her amazing? We'll all get a free boost in serotonin in our brains...so we can all come to group to get high!"

They loved it. I let Juan pick who would be confronted on their greatness this time; he picked Mike. The first kid to raise a hand to give Mike feedback was Daquante, a hardcore street kid from D.C. who's used to carrying a gun and being part of a gang. As he started telling the class about Mike's greatness, I stopped him and said, "Turn to Mike and tell Mike, not the class, what makes him amazing. Tell him, 'Mike, what I think makes you amazing is...'"

Daquante started, then stopped. "I can't do that," he said, "It's weird." I told him, "I know how strong you are...I know you can handle it." And once he gave the recognition directly to Mike, I gave Daquante recognition for his ability to handle those weird feelings like a champ. That broke the ice, and everyone followed his lead and gave sincere recognition to Mike's greatness.

Tammy sent an update to these episodes that illustrated how the habit of peer energizing almost always leads to student energizing of teachers and other staff members:

We now start every class/group with "lighting someone on fire" by telling them directly what we think makes them amazing. The kids seem to look forward to this and truly "get high" in group (they love this terminology).

Yesterday, one student asked if the class could set the staff in the classroom 'on fire.' During the rest of the 90-minute group, whenever other staff members passed through the room, the students would stop them and light them on fire. With each one, the intensity of the flames grew higher and higher. When the last of these staff members came through, there were only two minutes left before the bell rang, but eight different students AND another staff member took turns telling him what they think makes him amazing.

The givers became choked up. The receiver's eyes welled up in front of all the kids. Eventually, his eyes overflowed with tears. All the kids were sitting there silently, just taking in the whole experience.

The best part was that, during this last staff member's time being energized by his students and colleagues, the bell for dismissal had already rung. Not one student shuffled a paper, tried to get up out of a seat or even made a sound that distracted from what was going on. We were all about 10 minutes late leaving the classroom...and they all left the class as high as kites!

Supporting Children in Handling Strong Feelings

When you set the intention to reinforce a child for handling her feelings well, a whole additional vocabulary becomes available to you. Here's one example from an early childhood educator:

A few weeks into the school year, Matthew's mom approached me about his ongoing anxiety and fears, wondering if I had any suggestions. He had some difficulty with separation at drop-off time, but I hadn't noticed anxiety throughout the rest of the day. I told her we would make drop-off quick to avoid anxiety build-up and that I would make a point of giving him time to collect himself, letting him know that I trusted he would be fine and that he would join us when he was ready. I said I would point out his braveness and courage.

We had just finished up a unit on feelings. In it, I had talked about how all feelings are important and that if you're sad, mad or angry, it's great that you can feel that feeling. "When you're ready," I added, "you can be done with it and back to your happy self again."

One day, Matthew's mom spent more time than usual talking with me during drop-off time. I could sense Matthew's anxiety building as Mom remained in the classroom. Seeing his distress, I asked whether he'd like to read a story, and we found a book about an angry child. I pointed out all the feelings in the story, and by the end, Matthew was ready to join the rest of the children.

Near the end of the day, Matthew's hand went up during group time. He told the class about how he had been really sad that morning when his mom had left. I asked him how he handled those strong feelings; he shared that we'd read a book. "How did you feel after that?" I asked him. "Happy!" he answered. I then acknowledged Matthew for handling his strong feelings so appropriately...he was beaming from ear to ear! What a powerful download of braveness he gave himself that day.

Whether it's an anxious preschooler or a tough-as-nails, angry high-schooler, my experience bears out that acknowledging a child in the moments he is handling emotions powerfully and well has dual benefit. It is a tremendous way to connect with and honor the heart of a child, and it is also a superb way to be appreciative.

Children who have intense emotions come to see that they can love their emotions instead of being afraid of them—that, indeed, they can *play* with their life force and intensity. (The mother of a once difficult child overheard him saying to a friend one day that he had to "modulate his intensity" before proceeding with an activity.) Instead of medicating intensity away, we nurture the child's ability to use it positively.

If you have trouble allowing yourself to deeply feel your emotions, you're certainly not alone. Difficulty with strong emotions like anger, fear, sadness and grief underlie most addictions and life struggles. So many of us avoid feeling our feelings because we were inadvertently taught that we couldn't be trusted to handle them. We were told to stop crying, to stop being angry, to not be afraid, and as a result, many of us emerged from childhood afraid of strong or difficult feelings. That's just how parents did it when most of us were children. So we grew up and learned that it was best to ignore, suppress or bypass our feelings if they seemed too threatening—often by 'self-medicating' with addictions, alcohol, antidepressants, overeating, shopping or any number of other distractions.

Relationships suffer when feelings are not felt and addressed. Individual lives remain broken when one runs scared from feelings or attempts to suppress them. To be truly healthy, human beings must learn to consciously feel what's true for us and use that to navigate and negotiate our worlds—without letting those feelings run our lives as subconscious forces. As parents and educators, we have the opportunity to create a new generation of kids who can feel their feelings adeptly and see them as guides and keys to crucial information otherwise unavailable when they are covered over. And most pivotally, we have an opportunity to teach children to trust in their own power to manage these emotions well when they do come up. This approach is a great tool toward this end.

Following is a short (definitely not comprehensive!) list of feeling states. Use it as a reference to identify and honor students who are feeling their feelings and handling them in great ways.

If this list seems overwhelming, pick out a few of what you see as the most fundamental emotions: fear, anger, sadness, joy, wonder, and determination are a few good ones with which to start. The extent of your vocabulary around defining emotions is less important than the heartfelt honesty of your observations and acknowledgements. Keep it simple and truthful and the rest will take care of itself.

Feelings/Emotions to Recognize

Acceptance	Disappointment	Homesickness	Regret
Agitation	Discontent	Honor	Remorse
Alarm	Disgust	Hope	Resentfulness
Amusement	Delight	Horror	Sadness
Anger	Determination	Humility	Satisfaction
Angst	Distress	Hurt	Shame
Annoyance	Doubt	Impatience	Shyness
Anticipation	Emptiness	Indignance	Shock
Anxiety	Elation	Interest	Suffering
Apprehension	Euphoria	Irritation	Surprise
Aversion	Embarrass-	Isolation	Suspense
Awe	ment	Joyfulness	Sympathy
Bitterness	Empathy	Jealousy	Terror
Boredom	Enjoyment	Loneliness	Tiredness
Bewilderment	Enthusiasm	Love	Troubled
Betrayal	Envy	Modesty	Trust
Calm	Ecstasy	Misunderstood	Understanding
Cautiousness	Fear	Rejection	Vulnerability
Closeness	Frustration	Nervousness	Wonder
Comfort	Gladness	Nostalgia	Worry
Compassion	Gratitude	Panic	Yearning
Contentedness	Greed	Patience	Zest
Confidence	Grief	Peacefulness	
Confusion	Guilt	Pride	
Courage	Happiness	Rage	

Amanda's Story

At Cooley Middle School, this approach has not only supported the "greatness kids" who mentor and lead other students, it has also had a profound impact on the children who came to the school burdened with problems and more intensity than they could handle.

Amanda was just such a child. She came to Cooley engulfed in anger. She exploded easily and did all she could to drive adults away. Amanda had a learning disability but was obviously very bright. Her home life was difficult but she had adopted a caregiving role at home. Child Protective Services had been in and out of the picture.

Amanda had experienced a lot of things no child her age should. The staff at Cooley knew this child's story, and they were resolved to show Amanda that there was much more to her than difficulty and trauma.

"She would do anything she could to get us to ask her, 'Are you OK? What's up?'" school psychologist Mary Martin explained. "She might tear her paper up just as one of us adults walked by or do and say all kinds of other bizarre things. We refused to energize it."

"I would tell her outrageous things to energize her in any moment she stopped acting out," Celeste Elsey, special ed teacher, added. "I'd say things like, 'Thank you for not yelling,' or 'I see you aren't damaging your textbook right now.'" (In other words, she put the rope at the bottom of the pool.) "We were relentless."

During our visit to Cooley, which took place about a year after Amanda began to attend the school, Amanda agreed to an interview. She sat at a long table with a group of adults, including me, this book's co-author Melissa, current school psychologist Mary Martin, special ed teacher Celeste Elsey, former school psychologist Stephanie Rule, and math teacher Cari Prater. Our hope was to have Amanda share her thoughts and feelings about the past year. She jumped right in on the conversation and asked Mary, "Just how did you feel having me in your room, the way I used to be?" Mary responded, "What an intelligent and sensitive question. I knew you had a lot of reasons to be angry. You're a different kid now." "How were you before?" Melissa asked her, to which Amanda responded: "Mad. I would do almost anything to get attention. I come from a long line of people with tempers. Then I learned I don't have to be mad to get attention. It's not just the teachers here; anyone here will treat you like you're their own kid…they saw my greatness. I admit I used to take my anger out on people. Now I know it hurts me more than the other person."

"She has become this *light*," interjected Cari. Amanda went on, "You haven't just been teachers—you've been friends. Life is better here than at home…happier. Now I know I'm going to be better than my family. I love them but I have to do something bigger. I have a lot of plans," she told us. "I'm going to graduate from high school and go to college. I'm going to open a bike shop. My dad has just a GED and my mom has nothing, but I'm determined to get my degrees."

"Determination is a great quality that you radiate, Amanda," I pointed out. Amanda went on, "All I know is that these teachers, this school are the greatest thing that's ever happened to me and I thank God for it. If it weren't for them, I'd still have my mind in nowhere, not knowing what I'd do."

Here was a seventh-grade child, coming out of a childhood that could have easily destroyed her, who seemed to have more insight into herself than many adults do. Her genuineness and eloquence amazed every adult in the room.

"I now look forward to my future," Amanda said.

Adding the Greatness Piece

Seeing and reflecting greatness in a child 'in the moment' brings the child to an understanding of his own worth, value, ability to be loved and ability to contribute. It is an expression of the educator's deep conviction that each child is a repository of greatness that expands, grows and develops new facets when called out.

What makes the Nurtured Heart Approach work is that the student has an in-the-moment experience of being successful, of being in her true power and in control. Giving further recognitions that tie into the child's intrinsic greatness turbo-boosts these experiences into an even more spiritually nourishing dimension.

When you use the techniques of the Nurtured Heart Approach to shine the light on greatness, students gain clarity about who they really are: a core of greatness upon which they can rely as a guiding force in their lives. An intact, ever-expanding core of greatness is not impeded by self-doubt, fears and worries. A child comfortable with this core is not stopped by problems.

If you were sending positive recognitions to students via e-mail, adding in the greatness boost would be like adding an attachment that describes some way in which the child's choices reflect greatness. The child reads the e-mail, then (figuratively) opens the attachment to find out how you, the person of greatest importance in the room where she spends so much time, regards her choice as an expression of greatness.

To add the greatness piece with any of your students, attach an extra statement to your recognitions that pertains to the greatness that has always been at his core. In doing so, you give incontrovertible evidence that he's living out aspects of his greatness. For example:

"Timmy, this is a complicated project, and you have made choice after choice to stick with it. You are being disciplined and putting forth your best effort, and these are all aspects of your greatness."

"Evan, when Samantha grabbed that pencil away from you, you didn't grab it back or get aggressive, even though that looked frustrating. Incredible restraint. I've just got to accuse you of being a tolerant friend and classmate! Restraint and tolerance are great qualities and I see them in you."

"Lisa, thanks for coming clean and telling me the truth about this situation. Your honesty is a great quality and an inspiration to everyone in the class."

Stay in the moment. Find ways to 'accuse' the child of being great *right now.* Not only *can* she do it, she *is* doing it, and the evidence is right there, being spoken by *you,* the most powerful person in the room.

When the child is experiencing intense emotion, we can add the greatness piece to help her see that her emotions—although sometimes difficult to handle—are her allies in realizing important truths about herself and in making tough choices. We observe and reflect the child in the midst of a strong feeling state and describe how the child is exhibiting power and self-control. Some examples:

"Ginger, I could see that those boys were giving you a hard time, and you got pretty angry with them. I also see that you are handling your frustration well—you're being powerful by expressing what you are needing while still keeping your cool. That power is part of your greatness."

"Maria, you're so excited about the school carnival! Your happiness is lighting up the whole room. You're being enthusiastic and open with your feelings. Those are great qualities."

"Henry, I can see that you are bored right now. You've finished your work and there's still 10 minutes before the bell, but you're handling that boredom so well. You aren't getting out of your seat or striking up conversations with the kids around you. You're helping to keep the room quiet for those who haven't completed their work yet. You have self-control and consideration for others. Both are qualities of your greatness."

"Manny, I see you're sad about not getting a medal in the art contest. I see that you're letting yourself express that sadness, letting those tears flow! It takes bravery and sensitivity to let yourself cry. Bravery and sensitivity are great qualities that you have."

With a musician friend, John Frick, I wrote a song called "Stand in Your Greatness." I've been blasting it at the morning openings of my Advanced Trainings and after breaks to call the group back in. At one training held the year the song was created, quite a few participants found themselves dancing hoe-down style up and down the conference room aisle to this catchy tune.

This phrase, *stand in your greatness,* has become an important foundation of the Nurtured Heart Approach. I'm asking you to let your students stand in their greatness—knowing that some will resist more than others. Tell yourself: *this is not going to be a fair contest.* No child can prevent you from giving him or her a compliment! You're going to show them that you see their greatness. Nothing can stop you. The greatness piece takes Stand 2 (the "absolutely YES" stand) to the next level.

Bringing the recognition of greatness to your students is a YES at the level of the soul.

When I'm giving a compliment or appreciation at this level, I often feel time coming to a standstill. A timeless energy fills the room like a force field—a sense of the multitude of ways in which beings have honored one another all the way through time, coalescing in that very moment. As I look at the child and sense his energy, it is almost as if his soul rises to the occasion of the compliment, meeting my recognition with a corresponding YES.

Standing in greatness is something most of us must learn ourselves. It can be scary. It's an edge, just like the edge of a deep stretch. When you reach toward your toes to the limit of your flexibility, you may fear that reaching any more could cause strain. Although this is a concern with stretching of the body, it isn't with stretching greatness muscles!

In classrooms, teachers who are just beginning this approach often will give the appropriate nuggets of recognition, but they don't allow the students to really absorb them before diving back into the lesson. Choose to take a few seconds to deeply appreciate your courage and your caring in honoring these children, in knowing that their hearts count as much as their minds. Breathe into the 'stretch' and give just a bit more time to cultivating the light of greatness—in observing yet another few children as successful and honoring those moments. How much time does it really take? Twenty seconds? A minute? You'll more than make up the few seconds of time lost in your lesson with better focus and energy from students who have been given a reflection of themselves as great.

Let your intention to ignite greatness be as important as the lesson plan. Academic curriculum is the left foot and Nurtured Heart appreciations are your right foot. Go ahead and take a few little steps forward on your left, but take care not to let that foot get too far ahead of your center of gravity before you take some more steps with your right. You'll see that this new balance launches the trajectory of the lessons into a new vitality.

Chapter 6

All Roads Lead to Greatness:
The Nurtured Heart Time-Out/Reset

LET'S SAY YOU GET STOPPED by a police officer for speeding. He hands you a ticket, says "Have a nice day," then walks back to his car. At first you're annoyed, but then you look at the ticket. It's only a $2 fine! "Huh?" you say. Not so bad. You drive a couple more blocks and get pulled over by a different officer. Same thing again: "Have a nice day." No song, no dance, no relationship—just another $2 ticket.

You have a tight schedule and need to exceed the speed limit in order to squeeze it all in, so this keeps happening. It's taking time out of your day. What would most normal people do? Take a different route? Some might slow down and stop speeding. Normal people are fine with going 40 mph in a 40 mph zone, but you might have a level of intensity that drives you to feel that's too dreadfully slow. You might feel driven to live at 41mph and up.

If this is you, this isn't just a clean issue for you. You are not likely to simply change over to law-abiding citizenship in one fell swoop. First, you might need to go to the next level and see if you can get the officers off your back. Now you can't wait to get pulled over so you can try excuses or other rev-it-up machinations. You make it your mission to get your words in when you're pulled over again. But the officers do not engage with you in any way whatsoever, aside from handing you your ticket and saying, "Have a nice day!"

Eventually, the clarity and consistency of the whole thing gets just plain boring. You get that this new deal is here to stay and that there isn't a way of going around it. You might have been feeling a progression of frustration and anger up to this point, but now, out of clarity, you harness your frustrated, angry energy and use it to create a determined new stance. You cut back not just to 40, but to 35 to create a buffer zone, since you don't quite trust yourself right at the speed limit. You eventually acclimate to it and find that you are in control of the speed of your car in this regard, too. You are the one easing up on the accelerator and the one who compresses the brake and makes this happen, and it starts feeling kind of delicious. Undeniably, in the end, YOU deserve the credit for the turnaround.

This is the kind of consequence that works in the context of the Nurtured Heart Approach: the *clean time-out* (interchangeably referred to as a clean reset).

Where the Rubber Meets the Road

With the first two Stands, you will see changes, and they may be dramatic with easy children. Most of the children in your care might catch on very quickly to the fact that they can no longer expect relationship with you for any negative behaviors, but that it is abundant in response to all they do that's desirable and expected. Therefore, you may find that, with less difficult children, consequences are rarely necessary once you adopt the first two Stands. **But for difficult children, *limit setting* is where the rubber meets the road.**

Typically, the five to 10 percent of children in a school district who are undeniably difficult and resist other interventions will suck up 50 to 80 percent of the district's resources unless we can turn them around to an entirely different way of being a student. This next step is a pivotal one in this venture.

The child who believes firmly that he gets the most out of negativity will often go to the mat in affirming whether the rules of the game have indeed changed. Students now know exactly what happens when rules are *not* broken. You're creating a new realm of success, and your students may feel a little off balance. They may feel distrustful of the new flow of positive recognitions, but they like how it feels to be accused of making good choices. They are coming to trust that this flow happens when rules are not broken. They are learning to like the rules because they are absolutely clear and because they get recognized for knowing and following them. By appreciating students for not breaking rules, you have re-established clarity. You can rest assured that they know you know the rules and that you know they know them as well.

The stage is now ready for you to set limits. To do so, you need a true, clear, effective consequence.

Let's review the kind of rules that are necessary for this to work. Recall that when rules are stated as positives (be respectful…keep your hands to yourself…be kind), they create sufficient doubt to undermine the clear, effective enforcement of limits. How much disrespect officially crosses the line, and at what point is it taken to task? Such rules invite testing and pushing because the line between a rule followed and a rule broken is fuzzy at best. Positive rules also invite lectures, pep talks and warnings—all of which energize negativity—from the adults who can't really know where the line is with absolute certainty, either. When a child breaks or threatens to break the rule of "be respectful," the educator's response is generally to say things like, "I need you to be more respectful…the way you're behaving is *not* respectful." Meta-message: You are *lacking*, you are *falling short*, you are *not great*. Meanwhile, the child is getting rich, intimate relationship with you through negativity.

Think of a referee in a sport like football, basketball or soccer. Rules in these games are stated almost exclusively in the negative, and it's clear whether and when those rules have been violated. Refs don't spend time lecturing a player about how or why the rule was broken, or about how following the rules is just a better thing to do, or about how he'd better not do that again. A penalty is given and the game goes forward. This amounts to an un-energized time-out.

Refuse to energize broken rules; instead, strive during moments where the child is following the rules to acknowledge this with the techniques of Stand 2. You are showing the child, despite the past, that he not only *can* follow the rules and demonstrate great values and qualities: he *is* doing so, right now, in this very moment.

Here are a few examples of rules in the negative. It's helpful to throw in a few that you know in advance hardly ever get broken to provide even greater leverage in creating successes.

No lying	No being disrespectful
No stealing	No teasing
No aggression	No whining
No yelling	No bullying
No name-calling	No disobeying
No bad language	No distracting behaviors
No arguing	No irresponsibility

Educators often ask whether they should levy consequences only for rules that have been added to the 'official list' and discussed beforehand with students. It seems unfair to them to consequence for something when the student didn't know it was a rule.

My response: Do you see the rules of the basketball game posted on the sidelines, with players peering at them during breaks? Are the rules of the road posted on the dashboard of each car? Rules guiding decent school behavior have not changed substantially for the past century (rules about cell phones, mp3 players, dress codes and weapons notwithstanding). Just as the players and spectators know the rules of the game, and just as drivers know the rules of the road, kids know the rules they are expected to follow. And remember also our earlier metaphor about video games—players just jump into the game and learn the rules experientially as they play.

If *you* are clear about whether the child has broken a rule, that's what matters. Consequences for breaking a rule are non-punitive in this approach; you therefore needn't worry about harming the innocent. If a child argues against a consequence, saying that she did not, in fact, break a rule, do not discuss it until the student has reset and has been energized for it. You can then 'explain' the rule-breaking incident using Proactive Recognition. Similarly, any warnings you give about breaking rules will come in the form of Proactive Recognitions—where you energize children for *following* the rules.

For example, let's say Yasmin is talking and giggling with her neighbor while you give instructions for an assignment. "Yasmin, reset." If she does her reset, you can then jump right back with a Proactive Recognition (also a time-in) such as, "Yasmin, right now you are not being disrespectful. You are looking me in the eye and giving me plenty of wonderful, focused attention while I talk to you. Great demonstration of respect."

If she refuses because she does not think she has broken a rule, either move on to whatever consequence is designated for refusing a reset (more on "When a Child Refuses a Reset" a bit later in this chapter) or withdraw your energy completely. Wait for any hint of a pause or change in her energy that moves her away from rule-breaking, and then acknowledge her for successfully resetting. Add a recognition that she was willing to reset even though she didn't want to and did not understand what it was for. She reset on her own.

This is especially effective with very young children. If Nico runs and hides under a table when told that he needs to reset, be purposeful in not giving relationship around this. Don't try to remove him; rather, just wait a few moments, then 'accuse' him of finding a way of resetting himself that worked for him.

The reset is really just the *illusion* of a consequence. It's simply a pause in the action, after which the child gets further recognition for choosing to stop breaking the rules. The purpose of this consequence is to re-launch the child's new software of awareness of success and subsequent accrual of inner wealth. This is a different way to play hardball, and it wins the day in the long run—despite its brevity. When used properly, this short consequence works on the toughest children and even works beautifully with teenagers. Children see that we no longer look the other way when a rule is broken, and we don't accidentally 'reward' the negativity of the rule being broken. Rule-breaking becomes just plain boring.

Giving Students Permission to Break Rules

At this point, you might be thinking, *I hope no child in my classroom ever breaks a rule again so that I don't have to give this stupid reset!* But this approach requires that educators get out of the way and allow children to break rules.

Rule-breaking is not something to be avoided at all costs through warnings and second chances; rather, it's an important experience for children to have. It's an integral part of their job description! Children know that they have a choice when it comes to rule-breaking. As the educator, your role is not to prevent them from breaking rules, but to demonstrate to students that they won't be getting energized for that choice any longer. It follows, then, that only by breaking rules do they have a chance to see that what was once upside-down energy is now right-side-up. They now need to know experientially that things have changed—that accountability happens without the old sidecar of relationship and that relationship now happens only around success. You might even tell your students, "Go ahead and break any rule you want! I will let you know how appreciative I am when you don't, and when you do break a rule, I'm just going to give you a simple reset. You don't have to go anywhere or doing anything else. I'm unavailable during a reset, and when it's over, I'll turn back to you and appreciate that you are not breaking rules anymore."

Following an explanation like this, your well-behaved students might be the first to test you as they wonder if this new approach to rule-breaking applies to them as well; one rule broken followed by a reset will satisfy them. Challenging kids will try to rattle your cage and shake you off course. And **this is what we want: for children to go mining, hunting and pecking for relationship around negativity, only to realize they come up empty.** They end up bored, looking for a new realm—which you've already set up in the form of giving energy for success.

The difficult child resists placing trust in this new realm of positivity, but he also finds himself more and more drawn to it—especially as his old trusted partner, negativity, continues to fail to produce results. Once he sees how he can benefit, he comes to want to achieve as many points as possible in this new game of greatness.

Don't warn students that they'll be reset if they keep moving in the direction of breaking a rule. Resets don't need to be warned against! They are not punishments; they're a chance to remember to live out greatness. Besides, warning children not to break rules is like hanging a neon sign above your head that says, "My goat can be gotten."

Children are so relieved when they find they do not have to be perfect and that it's not a big deal if they break a rule. If you play your cards right, students will come to a point where they absolutely refuse to break rules.

Remember: It All Starts with the Time-In!

Address problem behaviors in a consistent, reliable way with the methods of this approach. Do so in a way that does not draw energy into negativity but allows the bright light of positivity to remain the strongest force in the room. A consequence that is brief and immediate and is over as quickly as possible fits that bill.

Begin by re-committing to the first Stand. Withdraw as much of your energy, emotional attachment and effort as you possibly can from dealing with students' problems. The following story from early childhood educator Pat Bethke is a perfect illustration of how powerful application of Stands 1 and 2 can preclude the need for consequences altogether.

On the first day of the new school year, I was eager to get a challenging group of kids in hopes of proving to myself how this curriculum of

106

relationship and building inner wealth creates a peaceful, respectful and cooperative environment where every child learns and thrives. After a very difficult separation from his mom, three-year-old Tommy entered the reading area. Once he had made sure I had noticed him, he picked up the beanbag chair, looked me straight in the eye, and threw it out into the room. As I turned my back and took my energy away from him, I reminded myself: no leaking negativity. I'm the prize. *I knew my challenge had arrived.*

My director, who knew little of the Nurtured Heart Approach but was supporting me in my decision to use it, had stopped in several times those first few weeks. Since she had not done this during her previous four years as director, I assumed she wanted to see for herself what this approach was all about. On this day, with the director looking on, I rounded the children up for group time. Tommy chose to sit directly in front of me. He sat very, very close, got up on his knees, and tried to get my attention by waving his arms and head around. He wasn't exactly breaking any rules, but he was pushing the boundary for sure.

When he finally realized I was not going to acknowledge his negative behavior, he stood up and walked over to the blocks in front of our group area. At this point, all of the children who were still seated turned their heads to look at Tommy.

With my director looking on and all the children's focus and attention turning to Tommy, my heart began to race. I told myself, trust the approach, *and looked calmly at a child still seated. To him I said, "I see you sitting and listening; you are being respectful and focused; and you're showing me what great control you have." As I continued to point out what great control and focus they each possessed, slowly, one by one, each child began turning his or her attention away from Tommy and back to me. Eventually, they were all looking at me and ignoring Tommy!*

Whoo-hoo! I'm the prize, *my excited brain said. But Tommy wasn't ready to give up. He pulled out a block and proceeded to put it on top of his head, looking around at every child. Not one of those little three-year-olds was willing to give him any attention!*

Soon Tommy put down the block, stomped over and sat back down. I immediately looked him in the eye and exclaimed, "And you came back and joined us! That is being cooperative and respectful...what a great choice you made! You are a great example to the whole class!"

This teacher brilliantly controlled the energy in her classroom. Despite her fear, she lovingly chose to refuse to allow Tommy to take the reins through acting out, then leapt at the opportunity to energize him when he made an excellent choice on his own. To do this successfully, she had to use her energy to bolster her determination rather than undermine it. She could understandably have been resentful or angry at Tommy, but she reset herself and was perfectly aligned with the next new moment when he came back. She stayed in the now and found it easy to express her appreciation for his great choice. And it was, indeed, a great choice; he could have held out longer or upped the ante through any number of additional acts of defiance.

Ultimately, resets would have made this situation even easier. Had this teacher been fully prepared to intervene with a consequence, it would have played out with all three Stands impacting the situation at once.

The Time-Out, Nurtured Heart Style

What we are aiming for is a **clean time-out**, meaning that **we are not dispensing a time-out + relationship.** The child gets a sense of missing out on life's privileges, payoffs and options—on the excitement and emotional and psychological nutrition now readily available when things are going right. **The clean time-out is boring and empty compared to time-in.**

Over the years, I have discovered that many teachers don't like 'time-outs'— for good reason. Traditional time-outs rarely work, and almost *never* work with difficult children, for the following reasons:

- Traditional time-outs are contaminated with energetic rewards (time-out + relationship); and

- Traditional time-outs are not offset with time-ins that pull the child into paths of success. It just isn't sufficient to draw the child away from poor behavior. If time-in isn't adequately rich, there's no game to get back to—nothing compelling to miss out on.

But chew on this for a moment: virtually *every consequence* most people can think of amounts to a time-out in the end.

Most of us are accustomed to two types of traditional consequences: 1) loss of privileges, and 2) restitution. When a child loses a privilege like her cell phone, her computer access or the ability to spend time with friends, she's out of the loop of life. Whether you call that a time-out or not, and whether the consequence is for 10 minutes, 10 hours or 10 days, in essence she is missing out on life's privileges. *Her deepest experience is that of a time-out.* Restitution might entail community service, tasks or extra work. What does it boil down to? A time-out from the action. Other kinds of consequences have this same end result, too. A child sent to the office or out of the classroom is in time-out, as is a child enduring a lecture about her misdeeds. All of these consequences remove the child from the energetic heart of the classroom for a period of time.

Some children will alter their behavior positively in response to traditional time-outs or other types of consequences. However, when they don't work, adults respond by intensifying the consequence: removing more privileges, giving more extra work or giving longer time-outs. By now you know that this intensifying will make things worse with the energy-challenged child as more and greater energetic involvement flow in the child's direction.

My favorite word to use for the brief, clean time-out is 'reset.' I like this word because it implies a pause...a re-entry into time-in that has a quality of restoration. Once the reset is given, watch like a hawk for any movement the child makes in the direction of stopping the unwanted behavior: even a simple pause can be sufficient. Once that happens, even for a moment, get right back to Stand 2—creating that rich, sweet time-in.

You can use other terms like "chill," "pause" or "stop"—whatever works for you and your students. Some teachers create non-verbal signals to indicate a reset.

Stand #3:
Clearly But Un-energetically Enforce Limits
(Absolute Clarity!)

Stand 3 of the approach requires absolute clarity about what the limits are along with fearless (but un-energized and un-emotional) administering of time-outs/resets when rules are broken.

The brief, clean time-out/reset (no lectures, warnings, explanations of why, or additional consequences involved) creates the result we most want in the moment, which is to get the child to pause while breaking a rule so that we can purposefully get back to expanding the portfolio of greatness.

How it's Done

To put a child in a clean time-out/reset, calmly and unceremoniously say the child's name along with some variation of "reset" or "time-out." If it happens to be a group of kids that are talking when the room is supposed to be silent, try saying, "Everyone in here who's talking right now, show me your great honesty and take a quick reset."

Once you've given the reset signal, completely remove your energy and relationship from that child or group of children. Do not engage in any conversation about whether or not a rule has been broken or answer any questions about how long the reset will be. **While a student is in a reset, no work counts, no questions are answered, and no one interacts with him or her in any way.**

Keep it short! For very young children, the reset can be literally two seconds long—as long as the child has stopped breaking the rule, you can welcome her back to time-in. No time-out should last for more than a minute. In practice, you will find that short time-outs work better than long ones. They make success less avoidable for even the most determined limit-pusher.

Keep it non-punitive! Punitive energy escalates connectivity at exactly the wrong time. Carefully withhold any sign that you have an emotional attachment to the child's choice to break a rule. Prepare to channel any energy you might have in abeyance into the return to time-in. Energize *yourself* for having the self-control this requires.

A student may get multiple time-outs during a given class period. There's no compounding effect of multiple time-outs; each is its own distinct pause, and each gives way to an equally satisfying time-in. Some teachers do have a limit on the number of time-outs/resets a student can accrue in a single day before stronger consequences kick in. Personally, I believe that if a child incurs multiple resets, it's not a sign to the teacher to get more punitive, *but rather to ramp up the first two Stands of the approach* to create greater impact on this child or children.

Make it predictable and boring. Be as vacant and detached as the police officer who writes a ticket and says, "Have a nice day." *Get out of the way.* Let children exhaust their repertoire of excuses, machinations and ploys. It makes perfect sense that they're trying them all. Consider how much energy they've expended in the past to either avoid a consequence or to exact the bittersweet satisfaction of gaining connection from adults.

As soon as the student completes the reset to your satisfaction, jump in with energizing statements such as: "I appreciate that you were able to get yourself to reset despite your anger. You were able to accept the consequences of breaking a rule—that takes inner strength. Terrific job."

If you want to follow up with a statement that will show the child how she has broken a rule, do so through a Proactive Recognition once the child has finished her reset: "Yvonne, you're choosing to work quietly now. I see you're still shaken, but you're focusing anyway. You're not getting distracted, which is great."

Be sure to give positive reflections to frequent rule-breakers when they are *not* breaking rules or threatening to do so. Otherwise, those students may begin to purposely break rules in order to get recognized for completing resets.

When students are seated, you can have them put their heads down on the desk when in time-out (some teachers like this as a reminder to them that the child is in reset); you can have them push their chairs back from their desks; or you can simply have them sit quietly without doing anything. The latter is my preference because it enables the child to momentarily experience the void of what she is missing out on, undistracted by any task or movement. The main point to remember is that *it's best to have students do the reset right where they are.*

The beauty of this form of resetting is that it is nearly impossible for the child to avoid completing it, plus it virtually guarantees a window of opportunity to "accuse" the child of successfully completing the reset, even if it is clear that the spiral of problem behaviors and poor choices is nowhere near done at this point in time. Even small breaks in the action allow you windows to purposely create more moments of success and more momentum in the direction of awakening greatness.

With the unwavering application of these time-out and time-in techniques, it is unlikely that a child will refuse to take a reset. If there are exceptions, give further consequences as needed, but know that detentions, placing a call to parents or sending a child to the office represent a slippery slope that can undermine the child's perception that no significant relationship is available in

When a Child Refuses a Reset

If a child flatly refuses to do a regular reset (we can call this a first-level reset), one option is to keep withholding energy as you wait for the issue to pass. Then, purposefully create the illusion of the reset having been completed. Do this simply by accusing the child of successfully resetting and moving on to time-in.

Another option is to move to a second-level version of the reset. This second-level reset should also stay in the classroom, but moves away from the child's normal seat. If you choose this route, carefully avoid any accidental focus on negativity. Just send the child as unceremoniously as possible to an alternative time-out location on the perimeter of the room. Some teachers do this by having the child face in a direction different than the rest of the class.

If the child still won't reset, the third level would be to follow school or district policy for a child who refuses a consequence. Ideally, office personnel and administrators in this situation won't inadvertently energize the problem, since they'll be on the same Nurtured Heart trajectory as you are.

connection with poor choices. It's better to ride out a few days of multiple re-sets while purposely notching up Stands 1 and 2 to find a level where optimal impact is created.

If district policy dictates added consequences or removal of the child to the office—any type of consequence other than the reset/time-out techniques presented here—do your best to ensure that such consequences are administered without the traditional 'crime scene investigation.' In this context, 'CSI' describes interrogation about the what, why, where and when behind behavior issues. As soon as a CSI begins, the child has succeeded in gaining connection through negative behavior.

Keeping Your Cool

Keep all consequences free of emotional reactions. The rules are just the rules. Reveal no emotional attachment to their being followed, and don't take offense when they are broken.

What if you're boiling with anger, fear or frustration on the inside? Don't hesitate to give yourself a reset or time-out if you need one, even if this means removing yourself briefly from an incendiary situation. Remind yourself that a child who refuses time-out is still convinced that she can wrangle you into energizing negativity. It's all about trying to have relationship with the most important person in the room: *you.* Such a child has a certain comfort in that zone and will strongly resist attempts to shift her to a positive portfolio. Steadfastly demonstrate to this child that **she cannot get you to violate your commitment to refuse to energize negativity, and she will come around.** You are taking stands that are unshakable. You are playing hardball. And it is a process.

Consider yourself fortunate if you have a child in your classroom who is determined to test this approach. It will push you to your own deepest commitment to intensely apply the Stands, which will, in turn, benefit every student in your classroom. Set your expectations high, have clear rules and reset yourself as often as necessary.

Remember that this approach is designed to "transform" difficult children to a new way of operating in the world. It is not an approach merely to gain a modicum of improvement. Improvements are good, but they always happen relative to problems—which means we're still squarely in relationship with those problems even when improvements are gained.

What every educator wants most deeply is to see the same intensity that was once problematic transformed into fuel for robust greatness. That's what we are fighting for with this approach. Holding tight to these Stands will get you to this extremely gratifying goal.

Safety First!

If a child's rule-breaking behavior threatens his physical safety or the safety

Notch it Up: *Reset Yourself as Often as Necessary*

At Cooley Middle School, every teacher and administrator teaches one of the E-period classes (recall that 'E' is for excel)—including principal Karen Calkins. Her E-period group consists of difficult students who are able to learn but who have been decidedly uninterested in doing so. On the day when I visited Cooley, she told me that class had been somewhat…out of control.

"I told the kids, 'If Howard Glasser walks in here right now, I am going to DIE of embarrassment. I'm supposed to be working miracles here and you all are going nuts on me! If he walks in and sees this, I am going to drop dead right here on the floor!' To which one of the students remarked, 'Hey, this isn't the Nurtured Heart Approach.'"

Karen went on with her story: "I asked, 'So, what *should* I be doing?' They gave great answers! 'You're supposed to get to my greatness before my negativity,' one kid said. Another said, 'I moved my seat toward you and away from those guys to get away from negativity, and now it's *more* negative close to you!'"

Students love to see teachers reset themselves. And this is essentially what happened in Karen Calkins' E-period class that day. She took a reset from her students, got back to her three Stands, and took back her power over the classroom.

I have no compunction about resetting myself as needed, even if it feels like I'm doing so a million times. Every time, it's about getting myself back to my three Stands and into as present a state as possible, regardless of what has happened in previous moments. The reset moves me back into acting and responding with intention rather than out of reactivity.

What works for me is deeply and efficiently feeling any emotional response to strenuous situations. Instead of going into the negative places these emotions can take me, I purposely use their wonderful energetic boost to further promote the tenacity of my purpose and intention—in this case, taking the Nurtured Heart Approach to an even greater level of implementation. It's a matter of scrambling to find the level where it all starts falling into place. If you hold to your Stands and keep notching it up, you'll get there.

Here's to the greatness of your tenacity.

of others, by all means, do whatever is necessary to stop him or her. You might end up energizing negativity, but your top priority is to keep your students safe from physical harm. Get your three Stands working again as soon as possible and reset yourself if you need to defuse any emotional residue resulting from extreme behavior.

Let physical violence or destruction of property be a signal to you to take Stands 1 and 2 up a few notches. Then, set up some form of restoration that will enable the child to make up for the infraction but that is void of discussion and energy; for example, some form of community service.

Make sure to complete the cycle of restoration by recognizing the completion of the consequence when it's done. Add verbal acknowledgment of the value and meaning of its completion. Also acknowledge the value of the actual restorative task the child was given.

For example: If the child was required to do community service to gain restoration for having destroyed property, energize the qualities of greatness expressed by the child in performing that community service. Do not revisit the issues surrounding the unsafe behaviors that began the cycle—other than appreciating that they are no longer happening.

With this third Stand, students awaken to the beauty of following rules not from fear of punishment, but from an awareness of themselves as great students and great people.

Introducing the Reset in Your Classroom

Although you can introduce the reset without any explanation simply by starting to use it, most teachers feel more comfortable letting their students know what this new consequence is and what is expected from them during a reset. You can also let them know how they will benefit from doing these resets well. They won't have to be sent out of the classroom or be lectured to; they'll get to keep learning with their classmates; and they will not have any privileges taken away. Tell students that resets are short, and they won't even have to leave their seats to complete them.

If you choose to discuss the reset with your class, be clear that *time-outs/resets are not punishments.* They are nothing to be afraid of—just a chance to check yourself when you're making an inappropriate choice or indulging unhealthy impulses. It amounts to an alternative way to plug back into the rules.

Keep Students in the Classroom

Sending a misbehaving student out of the room or asking him to sit in a special chair just offers another way for him to try to extract negativity from you by refusing. Even if he complies with your request to leave the room, he has an opportunity to put on a big show for his classmates while on his way out, which works against your determination to give the reset as little energy and time as possible. When you send a difficult kid out of the classroom to be dealt with by someone else, you are demonstrating that you can't handle him. It gives your power over to others. Most likely, he's already received a fair amount of relationship out there for the negative act that got him removed from the classroom. Even if the consequence that transpires out of the room is perfectly in keeping with this approach, when he returns, he's eventually going to act out even more, as if to say: *can you handle me now?* It will keep his cycle of acting out alive.

Handling the problem in the classroom will demonstrate to the challenging child that you indeed *can* gracefully (and without energy to negativity) handle whatever he throws at you. It will also help all the students see, through

Warnings Revisited

Throughout this book, we explain that warnings are a way of energizing negativity. Let's elaborate on this topic in the context of learning to use the reset.

When adults warn a child against crossing the line into rule-breaking, they usually believe they are being compassionate. Despite this wonderful intention, the reality is that warnings create a moving target. On a good day, a teacher might give six warnings before giving a consequence; on a challenging day, that same teacher might only give one or crack down immediately with no warning. How compassionate is this, really?

Warnings keep a child off balance. They sustain a lack of clarity about when a rule needs to be taken seriously. With warnings, the meta-message is that the rules aren't *really* the rules most of the time.

Warnings can undermine the first two Stands of the approach. As a student fails to heed previous warnings, frustration builds; along with it, the educator gets more and more charged and connected, thereby creating relationship around the child's choice to dance on the line between a rule followed and a rule broken.

It is far more compassionate to be absolutely clear about the rules— and to relentlessly reinforce the child whenever he or she is on the right side of the line. The only way I have found to achieve this total clarity is to steer clear of warnings altogether. If a child crosses the line, even a little bit, give an unceremonious reset and celebrate when the rule is being followed again. This reset is so simple and efficient, so utterly doable, that warnings become unnecessary.

their acting-out classmate, that doing one's reset successfully takes one to the other side of now: i.e., *success for both completing the reset and for subsequent positive behavior*. Keeping students in the room allows the whole arc of reset and restoration to take place in a few brief moments.

Some teachers have come up with brilliant ways to keep students in the classroom despite extraordinary ploys to extract negativity.

However, a student who does end up being sent out of the classroom can be told to write down five great things about himself or five good choices he made that day or three things he could do differently next time to produce a different outcome of his actions. A student who has caused harm may be asked to figure out his own reparations during the time spent outside the classroom. If a student has been aggressive toward another student, she may be told to write about the positive aspects of that student. This is all part of a slightly extended reset and meant to be purposefully energized when completed.

A Few More Guidelines for Giving Effective Resets

When giving resets, avoid energizing negativity and maintain clarity via the following:

- Deliver plenty of positives to students who are following the rules.
- Refuse to allow students to make any contribution to the lesson while in time-out.
- Refuse to explain the "why" of the time-out to the student or to the class.
- Refuse to take offense at rule-breaking.
- Refuse to shame/humiliate the rule-breaker.
- Refuse to use warnings or redirections *instead of* resets.
- Refuse to use warnings or redirections *prior to* resets.
- Avoid giving a time-out/reset in anticipation of rule-breaking that has not yet occurred.
- Broadcast resets to the whole room—not in a "gotcha" way, but at a vocal level easily audible to the whole class. Administer both resets and praise for all to hear.
- Refuse to make exceptions to the rules for students who have 'special needs.' This approach is for every child, so expect the child with ADHD, learning disabilities or other handicaps to follow the same rules as all other students. You will be amazed at how this changes things for the better. The child comes to accept that he is responsible for his own conduct and that he *can* adhere to the rules; and that when he chooses to do so, he gets plenty of relationship and respect from you.
- Choose to save your soul for all that you are grateful for and

appreciative of; and refuse to give your soul, the gift of your being, and the gift of your energy and relationship to negativity.

- Refuse, even when something has "gotten your goat," to let the child detect any energy related to that child's negativity. Instead, choose to feel those feelings internally, then use the energy of those feelings to notch up your application of the approach.

- Know that you WILL slip up (by sometimes energizing negativity and forgetting to energize positivity); and resolve to reset yourself when this happens.

Ending the Time-Out/Reset

When time-out is over, it's tempting to launch into lecture mode about the broken rule. This is where the adult usually blows it. End resets only by confronting the child with indisputable successes that are true of these positive post-reset moments.

When finishing a time-out/reset, do not try to get the child to apologize or promise not to repeat the infraction. Do not thank a student for completing a reset in a way that implies to the student that you are emotionally invested or that he's doing you a favor. Remember—the child makes the choices and the child gets all the credit. Acknowledge the student for her great choice to get the time-out over and done with right away; the good judgment that went into her decision; her self-control, good attitude and willingness to help the entire classroom be successful; or her willingness to get on task quickly so that she can return to making valuable contributions.

Let's thank Martha Stewart for this: you go to jail, you come out, you get in your limo, you get on your private plane…and it's all over! That's how I want to do it if I ever go to prison. When time-out's over, it's *over*. This doesn't preclude giving another reset in the next instant to the same child if another transgression occurs.

Here's a story told by one teacher who found a unique formula for the reset. She demonstrates how quickly a reset can be given and become ancient history in the face of the next moments of success. This story takes place in a classroom where the teacher was substitute teaching. The approach had not been implemented in that classroom, but you'll see how quickly it shifts things even when the children have never been exposed to it before.

One day, I notice Tony peacefully engrossed in play. He has constructed a ship made of blocks to transport wild animals around the classroom. Two boys come to join him, and soon I hear loud noise and arguing. In my classroom, we have a 'no arguing' rule, so I walk over to the group, which is already looking to me to intervene. Tony loudly complains: "They're taking my...blah, blah, blah....” So I hold up my hand and say, “Stop.” (No crime scene investigation for me.) As Tony continues to implore me for help, I repeat, “Stop.” The kids look back and forth at one another as though I must be crazy not to want to hear about the problem. I stay in the moment and say, “My rule is ‘no arguing,’ and I love how you have now stopped arguing! I appreciate how you all reset so wonderfully: so what do you want to do about this?” One of the two children who had joined Tony mentions that they could share, and in a moment, they return to their play. I give ample positive reflections, then walk away.

Five minutes later, the same group of boys is at it again. Once again, I put up my hand up and calmly say, “Stop.” They stop more quickly this time—they’re getting the hang of this—and I thank them for stopping. Then I ask, “How can you solve this problem?” The same boy answers, “We can share.” With this, Tony gets up and stomps away, and the other two boys happily take over his ship and continue to play. I walk over to Tony and say, “I really appreciate how you chose to walk away and quit your arguing. I love how you solved that problem.” Tony’s angry face morphs into a smug smile!

At group time, with all the children around, I honor Tony for how he handled the arguing situation by stopping, walking away and taking a break. I tell him he is a great problem solver. He smiles and nods his head. At the end of the day, during free play, Tony jumps up out of the blue, looking around the room for me. When he catches my eye, I notice he is playing peacefully with the same two boys, sharing the animals and blocks. “Hey, teacher,” he shouts with a huge smile, “I’m sharing!”

Tony downloaded two great things about himself that day, completely on his own: one, that he can solve problems; and two, that he’s really getting the hang of sharing.

In the classroom, resets are seamless. The interweaving of the approach into the school day is like this, too: *curriculum, curriculum, curriculum, recognition, this row reset, great job on the reset, greatness, curriculum.* When you take a great walk in the park or enjoy a wonderful afternoon of hiking, it all goes better when it’s left foot, right foot, left foot, right foot. If you take too many steps on one foot, you go in circles, plus you’re going to end up tripping over your own feet at some point! Mixing and balancing curriculum and character-building achieves a sweet, vibrant rhythm.

If you are resetting a student for refusing a request, be sure to initiate the request again as soon as time-in continues for the student. Don’t be afraid to give another reset for another refusal. One child whose parents were learning the Nurtured Heart Approach—let’s call her Nikki—had apparently, up until the age of 12, always refused to do her homework. Her parents were instructed to give a time-out, let it run its course, reset to positivity and then make the request again. Thirteen time-outs later, she sat down at her desk and did her homework with great diligence and purpose as if she had been doing it all along. Until that afternoon, Nikki's refusal to do homework had been a guaranteed lead-in to intense, animated emotional connection. The last hurrah was over. Now, the battleground had switched to winning the war of building great inner wealth. Her parents and teachers got to be joyful witnesses to her progression to more fulfilling pursuits.

Can Broken Rules Ever Be Overlooked?

When you are in charge of a classroom full of children, it can be impossible to administer consequences every single time a rule is broken. Under certain circumstances, like the one described in Pat Bethke's story about Tommy earlier in this chapter, the time-out/reset can be bypassed as long as the other two Stands are adhered to strongly.

The ideal is to give a consequence for every broken rule. Still, you may find many creative ways to wrangle rule-breakers into positivity without issuing a consequence by relentlessly energizing positives and refusing to give energy to negativity. This is especially true of children who are *not* adding to their rule-breaking behaviors or who are beginning to move back toward success.

An educator may be able to ignore a child who is breaking a rule when that child's behavior is not disruptive. When the child begins to solve her own problem, the educator is presented with an opportunity for positive recognition. In other words: **a child who resets himself can be welcomed back to time-in before any formal consequence is administered.**

My personal preference would be to provide closure and completion even when a child resets herself. Do this by stating, in the midst of other appreciations, "By the way, I appreciate that you found a way to do your own reset. You completed your consequence and got right back on track."

The Gift of the Reset

Think back to your own childhood when you were struggling to navigate relationships—something most of us learned on the fly, without any real curriculum to help us along this difficult learning curve. Wouldn't it have been wonderful to have a caring adult (or adults) in your life who, when you were spiraling out of control in some way, would give you a firm, gentle reset, refuse to reward you for negativity, and offer an appreciation for moving forward to the next brilliant 'now'? A loving message to stop, reconsider, gather your energy and intensity, and access your wisest and greatest self?

Learning to do this might have rescued you from a lot of angst and difficulty in your adult life. You can give this amazing gift to your students.

Notching it Up!
Nurtured Heart Clarity

When faced with a tough kid, I know it's time to notch it up. I start by breathing into the energy that's churned up by my own fears or resistance, and then I take inventory: I purposefully use the energy of my distress to ramp up the positives and relentlessly ignore the negatives. Then, I sharpen up the edges of the existing rules and bring in new rules as necessary. *Absolute clarity* is key here.

If I were to diagram this notch-it-up strategy, it might look like this:

1 Face off with a difficult, resistant child. Get ready to play hardball! Refuse to let the child in on your angst, visually or verbally — that's private.

2 Breathe into and feel the energy that arises in you.

3 Use the fuel of that very energy to ramp up the positives and refuse to energize negativity.

4 Take mental inventory of your rules; get crystal clear about where the "no" lies.

5 Use this new improved clarity to bring you back to more incisive and ever-deepening positives.

If you reach the end of this flow chart and the child still isn't responding, spiral right back to Step 1, using even more notched-up intensity and clarity than you did in the first round.

Hold on to your first two Stands, but be squeaky-cleaner about the "no" and use those rules to create the ever-greater "yes." As you cycle through this notch-it-up sequence, you are also:

- intensifying and optimizing this intervention by using the child's resistance as rocket fuel for creating the next 'now';

- breaking the child's addiction to pushing limits through total clarity around rules and a time-in limited only by your imagination;

- giving the child an incontrovertible message that resets are a certainty, but that recovery is inevitable;

- keeping resets completely empty of your connected relationship by removing the energy of YOU, then bringing all of yourself to the kiss of forgiveness and restoration by purposely recycling into the next round of post-reset successes;

- *expecting* the child to break rules and playing hardball by way of *no warnings* when he does; and

- seeing the worst child as the greatest gift who brings more and more greatness to the whole classroom.

Chapter 7
A Credit System for the Classroom

CREDIT SYSTEMS can work well to track student success and provide a tangible way to consistently recognize good choices. The creation and maintenance of a credit system may feel like too much to pack into your already full days—and doing so **is not a necessary part of the Nurtured Heart Approach.**

The credit system isn't something I generally recommend unless you already have one and want to revise it to fit the approach, or you are drawn to it and it feels right to you. It's true that some children do better when exchange of energy is made tangible in the form of points with which they can 'purchase' privileges. If you have issues with children who refuse resets, the credit system gives you a simple, un-energized consequence to fall back on. However: if you stay committed to the Stands of this approach, you can reach even those children without using a credit system by intensifying (notching up) the energetic exchanges that take place within your classroom.

Try not to single out one child for a credit system. If a credit system is mandated as part of an IEP (Individualized Education Plan), it may be best to take that as a cue to create a streamlined credit system for everyone in the classroom to keep things equitable.

Nurtured Heart Credit System Foundations

One very important credit system in the lives of adults is money. We all live within an economy where we receive credit (payment) for the work we do and where we choose to spend that money on things we want or need. Children have only indirect experience with the monetary economy, but most learn early on that privileges can be obtained in exchange for chores or that making cooperative behavioral choices can 'earn' goods or privileges from parents.

Parents commonly offer a privilege in return for compliance and cooperation: "If you eat your green beans, you can have some ice cream for dessert." Sometimes, parents will use the threat of withholding a privilege when the child does not comply with expectations or follow the rules: "If you don't brush your teeth RIGHT NOW, no TV tomorrow!"

The Nurtured Heart credit system is, ultimately, a way to add substance to the energetic exchanges of the approach. It creates a consistent economy for children by offering points or some form of 'currency' in conjunction with verbal reflections of their examples of greatness. It's just another tool you can use to build the energy of success and the breadth of inner wealth in your students—another way to systematically acknowledge their greatness in any increment in which it is expressed.

Don't give points *in lieu* of appreciative comments; they should only be given as a tangible representation of that verbal appreciation. Although the points themselves often become highly sought after by students, don't forget that these points represent windows of opportunity to deliver the main gift, which is connected relationship with you around positive choices and your expressions of appreciation and greatness.

Use a credit system that operates along the same principles as the rest of the approach: a system whose sole purpose is to energize the positive; that refuses to energize the negative; and that supports you in being as clear and precise as possible when rules are broken. This credit system will help prepare students for the real-life credit systems they will inevitably encounter later on. It offers them the experience of budgeting and thinking ahead about how to spend. It also aids in teaching the rules, as it offers credits for rules not broken.

To establish your credit system, you'll come up with two lists: "Ways to Earn" and "Ways to Spend." You'll also need to keep records of points earned and spent. Feel free to experiment with and streamline the system to fit the needs of your classroom.

How to Begin

First, be certain that your rules are clearly established, with as firm a line as possible delineating each one. Remember to include a few "giveaway" rules that all of your students follow almost all of the time so that you always have a reason to give points. You can choose to post the rules somewhere in the room.

Next you'll create a list of **Ways to Earn.** This spells out the many ways students can earn points and will include credits for rules followed and for qualities and behaviors you wish to promote within your students. To help with the latter, refer back to the list of Values and Qualities in Chapter 4 or the descriptions of inner wealth in Chapter 3 for ideas. You might offer points for being responsible, showing great effort, choosing to use good manners, sharing, cooperating, accepting "no" for an answer, following directions, using forethought, and assisting the teacher.

This system offers credit for any choice or behavior that could be recognized through the four techniques of Stand 2. When a child lives good values, expresses his greatness in a positive way, or chooses not to break rules, the points flow.

For each way to earn on the list, establish a point value. This value can either be specified on the list for all to see, or you can merely have the values in your head and improvise as you award credits. The latter method allows you to be more spontaneous in response to the moment. You may use the same point value across all the items on the list to make the system easier for you to use, or you may choose to assign higher points for items that you wish to emphasize. If your students tend to break certain rules more often, assign those rules higher points to motivate students to aim for following them. For example, if sharing and cooperating are issues for many of your students, assign those qualities a higher value. An alternative to assigning higher values for certain rules or qualities is to offer bonus points when those behaviors are exhibited.

As you figure out point values, remember to:

1. *Make miracles from molecules.* Look for ways to use credits to energize even small increments of success and expressions of greatness.

2. *Be generous.* Give points in increments of at least 10, which allows for lots of partial credit. (When points are given in all-or-nothing increments of zero to one, there's a greater proclivity for failure.) Hand out as many as you can.

Offer half credit if the child is working her way toward a better choice: "Greta, I'm going to give you five points today instead of 10 for the no-talking-out-of-turn rule. For most of the day, you waited your turn and very respectfully raised your hand."

When rules are broken, *never take points away*—**just give an un-energized reset.** Likewise, a student's refusal to reset is not grounds for deducting any points; it 'freezes' points so that they cannot be spent on privileges until the reset/time-out is done. The only way a student misses out on privileges is to fail to accrue enough points to earn that privilege or to refuse a consequence. Students are also not allowed to spend points when class work is incomplete or when problems are happening.

If a more severe infraction requires some kind of restitution—for example, if the child destroys someone else's property and has to repair the damage—points are frozen until that restitution is complete, whether through some sort of school community service, act of restoration or direct apology. The child can still earn points during that time, but he cannot spend them.

Again, **don't give credits in the absence of verbal acknowledgements and reflections.** Even if you use the credit system, do not back off on the recognitions given in the course of the day—the credits won't replace your energy and relationship given moment-by-moment in the classroom.

Any time you give points, also give a verbal explanation of the success behind them. With this in mind, use your creativity to keep your credit system as simple and streamlined as possible. Make positive recognitions throughout the day, but award credits perhaps only once a day. At that time, you can mention a few particularly outstanding choices made by the child that day.

Keeping Track of Credits

One method that has worked for many teachers is to use tickets, chips, play money, thank-you notes or tokens to signify credits earned during a day in the classroom. You can breeze by a child's desk, give him recognition and hand him a marker representing a certain number of points. This makes your accounting task much easier, while students experience the responsibility of holding onto those markers until they are ready to spend them on a privilege. I've seen the credit system serve as a great math teaching tool when teachers use markers with different denominations.

Ways to Spend Points

Once you have established Ways to Earn, it's time to consider **Ways to Spend**. This means that, whenever a student has earned enough points via the established Ways to Earn, the student can now 'spend' those points for whichever privilege she chooses. You may decide to limit spending on certain privileges based on times or occasions they work best for you. For example, if you offer lunch with the teacher, you would define when that would be available. Consider special activities, privileges or treats; create a rich 'menu' of choices.

Don't hesitate to make a privilege that was once offered for free into a privilege that must be purchased with points. One of my favorite creative privileges was dreamt up by a parent who allowed her foster son to buy an argument with her (arguing was against their rules). The argument could only last for a set period of time, during which the child got to say his piece and the mom got to energize him for being clear, eloquent and truthful.

One teacher created a beautiful "Junior Peacefinder" badge. The badge was hung on a lanyard, and wearing it entitled students to wander the room to give other students compliments. Though the privilege was costly, the time slots were typically sold out days in advance. It gave students a tremendous sense of the power of positivity—of the ways in which peer pressure can be used to serve greatness!

Below are a few ideas for individual privileges. Many of these ideas can have established time frames: 30 minutes of being a peer tutor, for example, or 15 minutes of extra art time.

> Assisting a school staff member
> Being a peer tutor
> Being a messenger
> Being the teacher's helper
> Choosing a sport or game at recess
> Choosing an activity or story for the class

Computer time
Correcting papers
Cruising the classroom offering appreciations to other students
Extra time with art materials
Giving the spelling test
Good report home via phone or note
Hall monitor privilege
Having special reading time
Helping in the cafeteria
Helping to decorate the classroom
Homework excuse passes
Learning a magic trick
Lunch with the teacher
Recognition/appreciation note to the principal
Recording a story
Small gifts (pencils, erasers, stickers)
Time to talk with a friend
Visiting with previous year's teacher
Visiting with the principal
Watering the plants

Group Privileges

A child may choose to spend points on a privilege that involves the whole classroom. Such privileges will cost more points than individual privileges. Any number of students might also choose to pool their credits for a group or classroom activity. Spending points this way can be lots of fun! These are ways in which students can energize one another; use your creativity to come up with others—they love it! Most only involve five minutes or less and provide a great break from the intensity of demanding assignments or curriculum. Some ideas for younger students from ingenious teachers (which can serve to inspire versions for older students) include:

Chair switching time
Chalkboard doodle time
Face making time
Free time
Game time
Giggle fest
Group appreciation fest
Group reading time
Group story time

Grumble and growl time
Homework excuse passes for all
Joke-telling time
Noisemaking time
Paper airplane time
Pencil tapping time
Recognition/appreciation note to principal from entire class
Quiet art time
School beautification
Singing time

Keep the credit system simple if you use it, and if you decide not to use it, know that you can still make this approach soar. It's no more than a vehicle to enhance your recognitions of students as great and successful, and a way for students to feel confident that their successes will be noticed on a daily basis.

Creating a Bridge between Home and School

The best place for a difficult child to have a credit system is at home, where most of her privileges are enjoyed and where parents can give far more focused attention than a teacher who is working with 30 or more students each day. Recommend to parents the book *Transforming the Difficult Child: The Nurtured Heart Approach* (see Resources section of this book) or the web site energyparenting.com. Both of these give detailed descriptions of the credit system for the home, along with other useful information that will explain to them what you're up to in the classroom. The Energy Parenting web site also has an online learning center on the Nurtured Heart Approach.

In cases where the parents want to become involved in the credit system, you may wish to use an individual credit system form like the one that follows to help the parents keep track of how the child is doing. The parents will have a steady flow of information about the child's school successes, which can be transformative in a difficult parent-child relationship. Simply request that the parents make a point of reviewing the form with their child each day and acknowledging and appreciating their child for a few of the successes listed. You can easily supply a sample list of the kinds of recognitions you are asking the parents to give their child. These extra efforts on your part to integrate the credit system with the home life could be a great start to motivating the parents to use the approach at home.

A Sample Credit System Sheet to Send Home to Parents*

Dear Parent of _____

These are the QUALITIES OF GREATNESS I saw in YOUR CHILD today...

From _____ Date _____

Parents' Initials _____

☐ Accepted being told "no"	☐ Kindness
☐ Accepted "Reset"	☐ Manners
☐ Attentiveness	☐ Maturity
☐ Caring	☐ Neatness
☐ Cheerfulness	☐ Optimism
☐ Compassion	☐ Patience
☐ Compliance	☐ Peacefulness
☐ Cooperation	☐ Perseverance
☐ Courage	☐ Positivity
☐ Determination	☐ Problem Solving
☐ Effort	☐ Punctuality
☐ Fairness	☐ Respect
☐ Flexibility	☐ Responsibility
☐ Focused	☐ Self-Control
☐ Forgiveness	☐ Self-Respect
☐ Friendliness	☐ Sportsmanship
☐ Generosity	☐ Thankfulness
☐ Helpfulness	☐ Thoughtfulness
☐ Honesty	☐ Tolerance
☐ Initiative	☐ Trustworthiness
☐ Integrity	☐ Workmanship

* *From the* Ten-Day Turnaround *by Susan McLeod at EnergyParenting.com and based on the Nurtured Heart Approach.*

Notching it Up!
Using the Approach As Though Your Life Depended On It

In situations where a child is willing to go to incredible extremes to extract relationship through negativity, I've coached parents and teachers to use the approach like their lives depend upon it. Sometimes, the truth is that their lives or the life of the child *do* depend on having an intervention that works, and when they begin to use it in this way, it finally begins to bring the desired impact. The mantra here is: **the more intense the child, the more intense the intervention.**

In the years since I've given up my therapy practice, I am sometimes contacted by a family in desperate need. They want me to work with them directly, and I often tell them that I can help them despite the fact that I no longer have an office or an active therapy practice. But I have one caveat: They must read *Transforming the Difficult Child* and put the approach fully into motion as if their lives depend upon it. After a month of using the approach, I tell them, we can have a direct consultation to help them optimize the approach for their child.

In the dozens of times I have offered this over the past five years, not one family needed to meet with me after that month was up. They notched it up to the level necessary to bring the child around.

Chapter 8

A Whole-School Approach: Bringing the Approach to Other Teachers and to Parents

IN THE LATE 1990S, elementary school principal Maria Figueroa arranged for a two-hour in-service on the Nurtured Heart Approach for her Tucson school's staff, faculty and administrators. In the days and weeks that followed, she carefully observed what was going on in the school's classrooms.

It was immediately obvious to this principal that the teachers who had, to some extent, begun to apply the approach were bringing about clear and positive changes. Those who had chosen not to do so were struggling with the same old problems. The greatest benefit seemed to occur in the classrooms of teachers who made the risky choice to abandon every other approach they'd learned in order to apply this new model without reservation.

Based on this evidence, she made a big decision. She called a faculty meeting where she made a point of energizing those teachers who had made beneficial changes. She then told her teachers and staff members that, based on what she had seen, the school was going to adopt the Nurtured Heart Approach across the board. Employees had a choice. They did not *have* to adopt the approach, but Dr. Figueroa made it clear that performance evaluations would be based, in large part, on how well the approach was applied.

This was an extreme step, but this principal's school was struggling. At that time, Tolson Elementary was a school with very low test scores, major disciplinary issues, bullying, high special education use, and high rates of psychiatric diagnosing and medicating of students. Eighty-plus percent of the students qualified for free or reduced lunch, and Tolson had eightfold more suspensions than other schools in its large district. Frustrated teachers resulted in an attrition rate of over 50 percent per year. She sensed that, by getting everyone on board with this approach, she could make big shifts, fast.

She was right. It took about a month to get everyone on board, and the shifts came, fast and furious. In every one of the areas listed above, vast improvements took place. In the 10 years since the Nurtured Heart Approach was first implemented, only one child has been suspended (twice). No new ADHD diagnoses were made and no additional children were placed on medications. Special education utilization dropped from 15 percent to just over one percent while the number of students qualifying for the school's gifted and talented programs saw a corresponding rise. Tolson went from having some of the worst test scores in the district to having excellent scores, and teacher attrition fell to almost zero. Bullying among students almost ceased.

Dr. Figueroa's example was followed by other principals, including Dr. Susan Zola of Jefferson Middle School in Champaign, Illinois, and Dr. Trudy Walters of Barkstall Elementary, also in Champaign. The 2009 Nurtured Heart Advanced Training hosted a handful of other principals and vice-principals exploring a whole-school application of the approach. The approach is also being explored at a program-wide level in psychology practices, foster care agencies, treatment facilities, community programs, group homes and the entire gamut of educational settings.

Other whole-school or whole-program success stories include these:

- At Tucson Head Start, the Nurtured Heart Approach was implemented in 1999, at which time 80 classrooms served 2,000 underprivileged children and had an entire mental health department to handle all the ADHD and other so-called mental health issues. In the first year of the approach's application, there was not a single additional diagnosis. So much money was saved on mental health services by using the approach (and with some additional funding) that enrollment was expanded to serve an additional 1,000 children.

- The Drenk Center, a foster care treatment center in New Jersey, experienced a reduction in broken placements to *zero* after implementing the approach center-wide. For years before that, broken placements had averaged 20 to 25 percent.

- Focus on Youth, a foster care program in Ohio with an average population of 70 children, reported that from 2007 to 2009, broken placements were reduced as a result of using the Nurtured Heart Approach in all modes of treatment and care. Utilization of medications by the children dropped to around 18 percent, which research demonstrates is lower than in many foster care systems in the US: one 2006 study found that 34.7 percent of foster children in Texas were taking at least one psychotropic medication.[1]

In most schools, teachers and staff are left to their own devices in terms of how to enact discipline and foster healthy relationships. School counselors are often required to run around putting out disciplinary fires, trying to help problem kids turn themselves around—but, in the end, they most often find that those kids keep making the same bad choices. Not surprising, in light of what you now know: that if a child gets to connect with a kind, compassionate person whenever she acts up—whether that person is a school counselor, administrator or any such adjunct faculty—it only reinforces her motivation to act up.

---

1. Zito JM, et al, "Psychotropic medication patterns among youth in foster care," *Pediatrics* Jan 2008; 121(1):157-163.

Many teachers who were ready to switch to a new profession find that their love of the job is renewed when they implement this approach. In 2009, Dr. Susan Zola, principal of Jefferson Middle School, reported that since school-wide implementation of the approach three years earlier, she has had to replace only one teacher—a big change from years prior.

The Key Role of Administrators

A unified approach is better than a scattershot one, no matter what that approach might be. No conductor would allow the string section to play rock, the horn section to play jazz and the percussion section to play reggae simultaneously. Even if those musicians are world-class, and even if they each play the most wonderful music on their own, they can't expect to bring different scores to orchestra rehearsal! Similarly, allowing teachers to take their own approaches to the hidden curriculum and to classroom discipline can create a cacophonous mess, no matter how brilliant the individual members of that school's "orchestra."

The orchestra's conductor helps all of his musicians sound their best by insisting that they play the same piece and that they do so according to the exact notes, rests, time signatures and dynamics indicated in the score. When a principal—the "conductor" of the school—has the philosophical backdrop and the conviction to promote or mandate a single approach to the hidden curriculum, everyone's efforts make more sense and have better results for students. Even if some angry voices rise in protest in the very beginning, teachers are happier and the school becomes a happier place when administrators take such a stance. It's hard to remain resistant when the shift happens and children start acting out greatness.

I've met many brilliant school administrators who believe in the Nurtured Heart Approach but nonetheless insist (based on perfectly sound reasoning) that mandating a school-wide approach is folly. The wisdom thus far among these leaders has been to start an inspired movement among the most motivated teachers, who in turn would inspire others. I have been privileged to watch this very situation unfold a number of times. Not only have these few motivated and inspired teachers clearly had an impact in tough situations, but many have been willing to go out of their way to share their successes and attempt to light a fire among their colleagues through presentations, discussions and mentoring.

Most often, however, these teachers, even with their great examples, do not fully light the desired fire in their colleagues. Those who are opposed to change, many of whom had the most to gain because of ongoing struggles with challenging children, often remain unwilling to follow the example of their fellow teachers.

However, in settings where an educational leader asserts himself or herself on behalf of the approach, teachers respond differently. When the conductor of the school orchestra declares, "This is what we are going to play today," teachers and support staff come on board. They may do so reluctantly, but resistance seems to dissipate when the boss uses the approach's positive recognitions with his or her own faculty, taking every opportunity to applaud those teachers for joining the 'orchestra.'

This all being said, I recommend that administrators begin by experimenting with the approach with a few teachers to see whether the approach matches the visions of the school. Schools like Tolson that are struggling are most poised to benefit from a whole-school mounting of the approach.

When the approach does feel right, the most positive impact comes when an administrator makes the leap to declaring, as did Tolson's Dr. Figueroa, that the school will adopt the approach from that point forward. Administrators must be willing to do everything necessary to mentor, support and inspire the teachers in making it work. For teachers who flat-out refuse to participate, the administrator can offer to help find that teacher a school that will be a better fit.

The Logistics of the Whole-School Approach

Some disciplinary approaches require a costly financial buy-in from schools; this is not one of them. There is almost no cost to a school aside from the purchase of books; and although it's beneficial for each person to have this book, even that is not a necessity. Schools also can hire a Nurtured Heart Advanced Trainer to teach the approach to school personnel, but the approach can also be taught to colleagues based purely on the information in this book. The approach can be used effectively with very little training. Even a less-than-perfect application will still have great benefit. When the whole school is using it, staff members support each other in developing their expertise and in staying motivated as they shift to a new way of seeing and interacting with students. Usually, the approach ends up having a positive effect on the way staff members relate with one another as well. The Nurtured Heart Approach can have great positive impact on the culture of a school—an impact that often carries over to the culture of entire school districts and their surrounding communities.

Schools like Cooley Middle School are even teaching streamlined versions of the Nurtured Heart Approach directly to students. These students are brilliantly applying the approach in their own lives; many are beginning to introduce this approach to their own families. In 2010, we trained our first Junior Advanced Trainer, a middle-school student who intends to share it with other student leadership colleagues. This young person has world-changing

Benefits of a Whole-School Application

The whole-school application of the Nurtured Heart Approach creates many benefits:

Endless opportunities for energizing between staff members, teachers and administrators. Imagine the work environment that is created when a school dives into the approach all the way. How supported, encouraged and valuable would you feel?

Staff meetings and IEP meetings that are celebrations of success. Instead of the forays into negative issues that can surround these gatherings, a focus on what's going right leaves everyone feeling accomplished and connected—and problems still get solved and work still gets done. Starting meetings with even five minutes of sharing successes changes the whole feel of the meeting. No one wants to miss even an instant. Subsequent topics take on an entirely new tone. Staff members begin to amaze one another with more collaborative solutions.

Continuity and consistency at various levels of discipline. For example, when a student is sent to the office or is given a detention, everyone deals with it without energizing negativity while continually looking for ways to energize the positive and holding on to the clarity of consequence.

Less need for students to be sent out of the classroom. Everyone tries to keep the child where he or she can get right back into the flow of positives (the time-in) as soon as a reset is over. Students who refuse resets can be sent to the office, but once the student arrives, the Nurtured Heart principal knows to send those students back to the classroom as soon as the reset is done. The student doesn't get evidence from the principal or any other staff member that he *can* get energy for negativity. You're all working to prove that this is no longer where the juice is.

Inner wealth building for students throughout the school day in the whole-school community. In the classroom, in the lunchroom, on the playground—students are confronted with incontrovertible evidence of their own success and greatness!

Students who are inspired to energize their teachers and each other. On many occasions in a Nurtured Heart school, I have heard students respond to invitations to energize one another or their teachers by pouring out heartfelt acknowledgements as though they couldn't wait to be asked. Many principals using this approach purposely make short visits to classrooms so they can tell both students and teachers about their greatness; often, they ask students to say a few great things about their teachers or their fellow students during these visits.

determination and vision. She's inspired me to begin to include elements in future trainings for young people who wish to teach peers.

Introducing the Approach to Fellow Teachers and Administrators

If you feel moved to do so, consider yourself a potential catalyst for creating this shift in your own school. If you are a teacher or a counselor, this goal is best reached by first getting an administrator on board.

Once you've experimented with the approach yourself for a while and experienced its impact, ask whether you can do a brief in-service. Having applied the approach for a while will allow you to share some actual experiences along with the conceptual framework and methods. Following the in-service, ask around to see whether anyone feels interested in experimenting with what they've learned. Follow up with anyone who wants to try the approach: provide support; recommend this book; and if the teacher begins to implement the approach, visit that classroom to offer feedback. Once a small group of interested parties has formed, they can join forces to approach an administrator about spreading the approach to the school community. At the very least, share this approach with your school counselor(s)—they are the staff members in schools who often are in the position to motivate and inspire others and often turn out to be guiding forces in expanding the approach through an entire school. I know of quite a few schools that have become 'whole-school' via the impetus of one single motivated person.

Introducing the Approach to Parents

It is the rare teacher who has not had the experience of meeting with parents over problems with their child. This is not a pleasant experience for parents, who might feel shame, hostility or helplessness over the situation—particularly if they are out of ideas about how to handle their child at home. The next time a difficult child in your classroom has problems, bypass the urge to call the parents for a meeting. Try first to create success right in the classroom by intensifying this book's recipes for the approach—in other words, notch it up.

My favorite way of introducing parents to the approach is to wait until the child in question has been exposed to the approach in the classroom long enough that you see signs of the approach's growing impact. Then, call or meet with the parents to discuss the child's successes. This is vastly different than the more common trap of calling parents only to inform them of problems. Instead of bringing the stressors of a negative message, you now have a genuinely positive message to share.

Use the moment to give the parent some credit and to begin to explain the fundamental tenets of the approach. Jump right in with the truth of this new now, conveying new success with the language you've been using in the classroom: "Mrs. Harris, I just wanted to let you know how wonderfully Evelyn is doing in my classroom. She is being cooperative, attentive and respectful and is responding so well to a new approach I am now using with the whole class. Can I share with you a little bit about what we're up to?"

Many parents dread any contact with the school. For some, this stems from their own personal negative experiences as students. Approaching them with news of problems can place them in a very defensive place. On the other hand, approaching them with news of their child's success can warm them into a wonderfully receptive and collaborative place.

Appreciate the parents for their part in the change and for their support. Energize the parents for being open to hearing about a new approach. "That's so great that you're right here, wanting to learn about something new that has helped Evelyn thrive. Essentially, I make a very big deal whenever students do something positive. I'm appreciating them out loud when they don't break the rules and when I see other good choices. And when they do break rules, I don't give them my energy. They just get a quick, easy consequence—a very short time-out at their seat that I call a 'reset,' and when it's over I get right back to applause for success." Invite the parents to come into the classroom sometime to see the approach in action. Don't get pulled into any conversation about the child's problems; keep resetting to acknowledgements of the child's greatness and the greatness of the parents as well.

The credit system form supplied in the previous chapter can help parents collaborate with educators in cultivating their child's greatness and get them on board with the approach at home.

Nurtured Heart Healing

The child who is constantly in trouble is constantly stressed. Faced with the difficulties he creates, he struggles internally. In order to have the intense relationship he needs from the adults he most respects, he believes he has to do things that bring disapproval, punishment, even shame. He may be shunned or teased by other children, which creates even more stress.

Stress is harmful to health. It disturbs the functioning of the immune system, creates a state of chronic agitation, and makes us more susceptible to a long list of health woes, including bowel problems, headaches, chronic tension and pain, depression and anxiety disorders, obesity and type 2 diabetes. A person who is stressed also is far more likely to engage in bad health habits (eating junk food, for example, or failing to exercise).

According to the experts at the world-renowned Mayo Clinic, a positive approach to life has many health benefits. Research shows that positive thinking may lower rates of depression and distress, improve resistance to the common cold, create overall improvements in physical and psychological well-being, extend life span, and facilitate better coping during times of stress. People who think positively exercise more and have less need for toxic substances (alcohol, tobacco, junk food).[*]

The Nurtured Heart Approach goes beyond the standard notions of positive thinking or a positive attitude. It provides tools for celebrating the greatness of every aspect of life. Even difficult emotions and coping with hard life circumstances can be cause for celebration. It's a kind of radical, relentless positivity, and it has profound healing effects.

Remember Amanda's story in Chapter 5 and Sean's story in Chapter 1, both of whom were students at Cooley middle school with serious issues although of a dissimilar nature. These two students are examples of how the approach can heal relationships and hearts that have been hurt by inadvertent messages that negativity and bad behavior are the most efficient ways to obtain compelling relationship. Stress hardens hearts; healed stress softens and opens hearts.

As the child is transformed, his burden of stress is lifted. His limbic system can relax out of fight-or-flight mode. He can reset into balance. The child comes to love his own intellectual and emotional intensity as he realizes that he can now control and use it in a positive direction. His

---

[*] www.mayoclinic.com/health/positive-thinking/SR00009

self-control feeds into new and positive relationships with cherished adults. His progressing sense of inner wealth will bring him to choose more kindness and support in his peer groupings and activities.

How about you? What level of stress are you forced to cope with when intense students act up in your classroom? How about stress at home— in your relationships with children, spouse or other relatives?

Although the Nurtured Heart Approach is a tool for helping children flourish, its methods often prove very useful for relating to other adults. I say this based on the feedback I have received from educators and parents from all over the world. As they've learned, applied and embodied this approach, even teachers who were suffering extreme burnout loved teaching again. They find themselves shifting to a more positive outlook toward their students and their careers. They find ways to relate more positively with their own children, their spouses and their co-workers.

Applying this approach to any relationship makes it far less stressful. When you begin the great dance of positivity with your students, your job becomes a pleasure and a lot of stress is lifted.

And, as you'll see in the next chapter, when you apply the approach to your own inner life, you can learn to breathe into and live in the healing, abundantly positive manner that is your birthright.

Chapter 9
Becoming the Approach

TAMMY SMALL, a counselor and superb Nurtured Heart trainer in Newcastle, Washington, presented a training to about 80 Head Start employees in late 2009, including Head Start's bus driver Sharene Forest. After the training, Sharene sent this note to Tammy.

At first I couldn't comprehend the subject matter. By the first break, I was thinking of all the reasons I could give my boss for not staying. I don't like it when I can't understand the material that's being presented…it hasn't happened often in my life. Shortly after the break, I asked you a question. My name tag had fallen off, and you asked my name and complimented me. That's when I got the subject matter. Nurturing the heart.

You said my name without faltering and you didn't forget it all day long. I cannot begin to tell you the impact that had on me. I got this tightening around my heart, this lump in my throat, as the impact of having little to no nurturing in my life hit me. Not only did I have none, but I didn't do a very good job of nurturing my son…who, by the way, turned out to be an excellent human being despite his upbringing. I was astounded by how many times I welled up in tears during the rest of that day. I am not an emotional woman.

Over the next few days, I thought about what you presented. Nurtured Heart so totally makes sense to me. I presented a brief explanation to my co-workers at our monthly meeting. They were so full of questions that I'm going to do a presentation for them next month. I will study hard and practice this method on my bus riders. It's difficult, as this is way out of my comfort zone. Nurturing means being nice and meaning it. My old rule to live by was kindness=weakness; my new rule to live by is kindness=strength.

I'm catching on quickly. My soul needs this. I already feel happier than I have for a long time. I've never had such an experience in my life.

You can treat the Nurtured Heart Approach simply as a method for working with students. The techniques can be learned and successfully applied without looking beyond the impact on individual children and the overall flourishing of your classroom. Such a way of using the approach is completely in keeping with the primary intention of this book.

However, if you feel ready to take steps toward creating a more joyous and passionate life for yourself, you can take this approach to another frontier: using it as an internal blueprint for moving through the adventure of life.

Sharene did this on her own, as do many others who learn the Nurtured Heart Approach.

Changing Your Default Setting

What if a child in my classroom throws something at another student…texts in class…leaves the room without permission…hits another child…insults another child…insults or disrespects me? Those 'what-ifs' are almost always about worries, doubts and fears, and many of us tend to steep ourselves in them—even those of us who see ourselves and appear to others as extremely positive. This mindset is so common and so ingrained in our culture that many who operate from it don't realize how this software creates an incessant gravitational pull to negativity. Success guru Jack Canfield has said: "*What if…?* are the two most dangerous words in any language."

And the other side of this potential quagmire is that we so easily attribute greatness to others: celebrities, public figures, entertainers, sports stars. Why not give our own greatness some air time? What 'soul-ware' (inner software) supports the 'heart-ware' (inner hardware) of greatness?

Greatness is in our hardware. I know this to be true when I look into the eyes of a child whom I am complimenting. In that moment, the greatness that has been in the student's heart all along shines clearly through. I can feel it 'activating,' like a new disk of software loading on a computer. As we learn to more energetically present with greatness in others, it feels natural and right to learn to do the same within ourselves. The techniques and intentions of the Nurtured Heart Approach can be used to consciously direct energy internally, toward our own greatness.

This practice of seeing and reflecting my own greatness goes directly against the culture that surrounded my own upbringing. As a child, I downloaded a clear message that I got more out of life through negativity. The worse things got in my acting-out childhood, the harder my loving parents tried, the more energetically fed that negativity was and the more confused I felt. However revolting this felt to me back then, and despite the greatness I now know was my birthright, this software was deeply programmed into my inner self. It ran my relationship with myself, and I manifested that negativity in my thoughts and ways of responding in the world.

This software, which was custom-designed through the experiences of my youth, persisted in the background well into my adult life. Later on, even as I was creating, using and teaching this extremely positive approach with children and families and thinking I was a highly positive person, a series of events led me to the energetic truth that I was still steeped in a private purgatory of negativity. By applying the Nurtured Heart Approach to myself, I met the challenge of changing my deeply ingrained default of negativity. In the process,

I recognized that the best way to make this approach work for others is to *live it myself*. I call this "being the approach." It's a daily practice I use to keep my own inner flame of greatness going and growing.

This dramatic transformation in myself is the reason why I can wrestle the world's most difficult kids away from *their* negativity. By way of this practice, I can progressively grow in my appreciation of the dynamic tension and intensity within even the most challenging kids, and I can see clearly how all that tension is set to explode into greatness.

Some of us have an innate positivity that serves as our 'default setting'—the place we naturally go, even when things get tough. If you are one of those fortunate few, you have probably had an easy time mastering the use of the Nurtured Heart Approach. The rest of us have a little more work to do if we're going to stop getting sucked into negativity. Our subconscious 'default setting' readily shifts our inner dialogue to problems, regrets, fear, worry and doubt. Shifting this undercurrent of negativity requires a plan for creatively, imaginatively learning to see greatness in ourselves.

WMDs 101

Energy is love, and loving energy causes things to grow. You've already seen this if you have changed the way you give your energy to your students. How about in your own life? Are you giving your energy to complaints, fear and anger? The same universal law holds true in you as it does in your relationship with students. If you give mental space and loving energy to your own fears, worries, self-criticisms and doubts, they grow.

When we spend our days stewing in what I call WMDs (worries, misery and doubts), we contribute to creating exactly what we *don't* want. This is why the very first Stand set out in this book is "absolutely NO"—a refusal to energize negativity. This isn't mystical alchemy or a New-Age spin on quantum physics. It's simply about *intention* and the power it has to form your experiences and your world. As psychologist, author and spiritual teacher Wayne Dyer says, "Change the way you look at things, and the things you look at change."

I hope that working with the techniques of Stand 2 has demonstrated to you that it is possible to change one's patterned, ingrained ways of thinking in a way that opens the door to vast possibilities. Making conscious choices to see the positive and to expect positive outcomes will positively shift your life. There's no magic to this; it's simply a shift in perspective that you can choose to enact at any given moment.

How much do you want to enjoy living in your reality? Your life? Your peers? Your work? What's your 'energetic reality?' Are you living upside-down energy as I once did, holding the belief that you are positive even as you energize what's wrong?

Being on the lookout for what's out of place has survival value. If you tune in to the beautiful flowers and trees instead of the oncoming tornado, for example, you may well not make it to see the flowers and trees tomorrow. We look for problems because we can then try to prevent them from ballooning out of control. In this respect, our automatic attention to problems is something to appreciate. On the other hand, this focus on what's wrong bleeds copiously into areas of our lives where it has no value. And it's easy to amplify our focus on the negative even in areas where it *might* count.

Many people live in fear about something that *could* hurt them but that is incredibly unlikely to do so. Some live their lives based on erroneous beliefs about what is and is not a threat to their actual well-being or survival. Using the Nurtured Heart Approach on ourselves entails becoming conscious of the stories we tell ourselves; seeing whether we're habitually defaulting to worry, misery and doubt (WMDs); making a choice to default to greatness instead; and doing so often enough and for a long enough period to change the WMD habit.

Cultivating Happiness Instead of Pathologizing Unhappiness

Our culture encourages WMD overwhelm. Increasingly, we've responded to these negative feelings by medicating them away. When it comes to drugs designed to relieve psychological stress, we've become the most highly medicated culture on the planet. In the U.S., we take more antidepressants, anti-anxiety drugs and ADHD drugs than any other nation. The U.K. isn't far behind, and other Western nations seem to be following suit. Seeing a therapist to unravel problems, fears and difficulties is far more common and acceptable today than ever before.

Psychological diagnoses are, to varying degrees, about *pathologizing* certain states of being. We go to therapy when something is wrong in our lives, and the focus during counseling sessions is on problems. If you're sufficiently fidgety and distractible, you're said to 'have' an attention deficit disorder; if you're deeply sad or numb, you are said to 'have' depression; if you are very worried and fearful, you may be told that you 'have' an anxiety disorder. If you are deemed to have these symptoms and therefore these conditions, the medical model's standard 'protocol' is to recommend medication. This is a slippery slope that often does not lead to the desired improvements. In some cases, medication ends up exacerbating symptoms or creating new ones that end up also being medicated.

Note how all of the focus here is on the negative: finding problems, talking about problems, crafting the best-fit diagnosis, and trying to examine and solve the problems in order to bring one back to some sort of neutral state—a state where one is "okay" and can handle life.

Positive psychology posits that we don't need to set our intentions on being just okay. We can set them on being fulfilling, thriving, positive and talented simply by changing the way we think and the way we view our world to reflect what's valued instead of what's negative.

The notion of positivity as a healing force in individuals and in society isn't new. Since Norman Vincent Peale's *The Power of Positive Thinking* was published in 1952, many have sought to explain to the world that thinking positively is key to happiness and good relationships. When you see positivity in action—whether through the Nurtured Heart Approach or some other method designed to enhance positivity—it's obvious that it works to improve relationships and quality of life for all those who are touched by the shift. Only since the early 2000s, however, have the methods for and effects of positive thinking been studied scientifically.

In 1996, just before positive psychology emerged into the mainstream, a researcher named David Lykken was hard at work at the University of Minnesota, trying to determine whether human beings are genetically 'hard-wired' to have a 'happiness set point': does each person have a baseline of happiness (or lack thereof) to which they will always return, much as a person will tend to return to a specific body weight set point no matter how much he or she diets? Are some people unable to change their default setting from negativity—and do others have a natural and unshakable positivity?

The study enrolled 4,000 sets of twins born in Minnesota between 1936 and 1955, and all the data gathered on them revealed that about 50 percent of one's satisfaction in life is genetically determined. That is to say, people are wired to have certain ways of dealing with stress; they may have higher susceptibility to anxiety or depression; or they may be blessed with a naturally sunny outlook. Lykken determined that about eight percent of a person's level of life satisfaction appears to be dictated by life circumstances (marital status, religion, income, education and the like). The rest, he determined, is under each person's individual control.[1]

At the time, Lykken concluded that trying to be happier "may be as futile as trying to be taller." Since then, however, he has retracted this statement, saying that "it's clear that we can change our happiness levels widely—up or down." In other words, close to 50 percent control over one's happiness represents a lot of control. This paves the way for the question of *how* to make one's life better and more fulfilling—a question positive psychology has set out to answer definitively.

Positive psychology scientifically studies the strengths and virtues that

---

1. Lykken D, Tellegen A, "Happiness is a stochastic phenomenon," *Psychological Science* 1996; 7(3). Available at www.psych.umn.edu/psylabs/happiness/ happy.htm

create thriving individuals and communities. It asks: how can we proactively create lives full of love, courage, creativity, curiosity, integrity and wisdom? How can we create more smiles and laughter, day to day? Positive psychology answers these questions through the study of people and institutions that seem to have found ways to achieve these ends.

Research on positive psychology has found that life circumstances don't have all that much to do with happiness. As long as our basic needs are met, extra wealth doesn't increase happiness. (Lottery winners often end up *less* happy than the average person.) A person who becomes paraplegic will have a substantial dip in happiness, but within a short time, that person's prevailing feeling tends to be gratitude for all he continues to have and enjoy.

Positive psychologists have discovered that, by counting our blessings, acting kindly toward others, appreciating even the smallest joys of life, appreciating our own strengths and the strengths of others, investing time and energy in friends and family, taking good care of our bodies, and having strategies on reserve for those times when things go wrong, we can maximize that 50 percent (or so) of our happiness over which we have some control.[2] Positive psychology is about finding what's right and enhancing it. In giving our energy to what's right, we naturally and organically remove our energy from what's wrong.

People who are more positive or optimistic live longer and enjoy better health. Even when they are less healthy, they have better quality of life than a person who stays mired in worry, misery and doubt.

I would like to believe that the Nurtured Heart Approach explores the farthest reaches of positivity. It incorporates techniques that enable us to find real evidence of love, courage, creativity, curiosity, integrity, wisdom and other desirable qualities *in the current moment* (as opposed to hoping for such qualities to be manifested in the future or looking back on their manifestation in the past). The approach also offers tools for *growing* such qualities in ourselves and in others. It goes beyond gratitude and into greatness…*great-itude!* Gratitude is certainly a quality of greatness that we can appreciate and energize, but so are many other feelings, qualities and values.

In both positive psychology and the Nurtured Heart Approach, specific techniques are employed to *change ingrained negative thought patterns*—to repeatedly prompt thoughts in the direction of greatness and away from negativity. Positive psychologists also point out that the more detailed our observations of what's going right, the more effective they are at improving our level of happiness. In the Nurtured Heart Approach, we employ as much

---

2. Wallis, Claudia, "The New Science of Happiness," *Time* 2005 Jan 17.; also, www.happier.com, Martin Seligman's positive psychology web site

detail as possible when acknowledging positives. The more detailed we are, the more convincing this positive feedback is to the recipient—and the more honest it is to us. We let the authenticity of convincing details wash over mind and heart, overriding the default to negativity. The Nurtured Heart Approach inspires (breathes in) the new default of success at the level of heart and exhales it back out to the hearts of others.

Nurtured Heart Approach techniques are also similar to those used in *cognitive-behavioral therapy* (CBT), which is often coupled with positive psychology in therapeutic settings. In CBT, the therapist helps the client evaluate how her thoughts and language create her reality—and how to alter them to create a more desirable reality. In greatness practice, we do the same thing, but in a simplified manner that anyone can learn without a therapist's guidance.

There's an important difference between CBT and the Nurtured Heart Approach, however: CBT is all about the mind, but the Nurtured Heart Approach is about mind and heart in equal measure. When therapists use this approach in their practice, they refuse to talk about problems. Imagine that: a therapist, whose job is usually to dissect and explore problems down to the core, refusing to talk about problems!

Just as a child who is convinced that negativity is the best way to get connected with adults needs a more detailed, intense and powerful application from the adult using the Nurtured Heart Approach, those of us who are more genetically apt to see the dark side of things might need a bigger floodlight to detect and produce a greater amount of positive details. In other words, we need a more intense and powerful application of the approach for ourselves.

If this is true of you, consider it cause for rejoicing. If, in order to shift from the negativity default, you have to go 10 levels farther with the approach than the next person, you're going to be that much better prepared to bring the very worst kids into their own greatness. If you have the inner power to be incredibly negative, you can transmute that power in the opposite direction and maintain every bit of its strength and intensity.

Changing the world really does start with changing yourself, but here, as my colleague Susan McLeod puts it in the Foreword of my book *You Are Oprah*, "It's not about changing. It's about choosing." You get to choose how you see the world and how you respond to it, beginning with the way you see yourself. This shift can be made through a distilled, self-directed version of the Nurtured Heart Approach that I call *greatness practice*.

Greatness Practice 101

This practice entails intentionally finding ways in which you are succeeding, right now, and taking time to energize whatever quality of greatness is being manifested in you during this particular moment of success. Whatever

Notch it Up: *Increase Your Impact on Students by Honoring Your Own Greatness*

Your only real authority is over yourself. Fan the flames of your own greatness; learn what that feels like; then give that gift to your students using the techniques you've learned in earlier chapters of this book. Your impact will be amplified.

This self-application of the Nurtured Heart Approach gives you real experiences of valuing the present moment and yourself in that moment, which in turn supports you in proving to students that their positive behaviors will lead to relationship success and that problems aren't necessary to forge relationship with you. I've used this practice on myself for years to reset my defaults from negativity, and I increasingly encourage those who are learning the approach to explore the possibilities.

level of pixelation is necessary, we go there to construe and create greatness.

If your life were a movie, you'd be both director and editor. Committing to the greatness practice is about stepping into this leading role in your own life and deciding to make a positive, uplifting film instead of a work that is potentially more negative in nature.

Those of you who have studied yoga probably know that it's not about getting to any particular goal, but about daily or near-daily practice; you never get to a point where you've perfected a yoga posture and never need to do it again. You return, again and again, to the same postures and ways of breathing, and you grow into a deeper peace and knowledge of yourself through repeated practice. So it is with greatness practice and the Nurtured Heart Approach: they are each a kind of yoga of positivity where you return, again and again, to the commitment to refuse to energize negativity (your own or that of others) and the commitment to acknowledge to yourself how you and those around you are exemplifying greatness in everyday thoughts, choices and actions.

A Crash Course in the Greatness Practice

Here, I'll offer you just the bare bones of the greatness practice. For the full story, refer to my book *You Are Oprah: Igniting the Fires of Greatness.*

Take a few days to practice each of the following steps before moving on to the next one.

1. **Begin to check in with your thoughts periodically throughout the day.**
   Notice how you talk to yourself. Do you speak to yourself as gently and

compassionately as you would a cherished loved one? Or do you most often criticize and talk down to yourself? Do you endlessly nitpick over what you're doing wrong or over problems? Notice how often you acknowledge yourself with enthusiasm for what you're doing right or for what's going right in your life. How intense is the energy of the dialogue when things are going right? How excited and emotional are you in those moments of rightness in comparison to moments when things begin to go wrong or when full-blown problems are in play?

2. **Think of the person you most admire—your favorite, most respected human being.** Then ask yourself: how is that person great? Make a list of the qualities you most admire in that person. Over the course of your day, see whether you can notice glimmers of those same qualities in yourself. Don't take anything for granted.

   For example: If your most admired person seems to have a lot of courage, find a moment in your day when you are demonstrating courage—even the smallest hint of it. "I am demonstrating courage in speaking up about the changes in school policy that I don't like." Or let's say you also identify a quality of compassion in your most admired person. "In sitting down with this student who is having trouble with his home life and being extra supportive, I am being compassionate." *You could not see any quality of greatness in that person you admire without possessing some level of that same quality yourself.* It wouldn't even register. Once you discover these qualities in yourself, think of them as flames that need fanning and consider fanning them as though your life depended upon it.

3. **As you begin to energize your own positive qualities and choices, also notice when you fall into self-critical thoughts, worries, doubts or unfounded fears.** When this happens, simply reset yourself and seek out the next great quality you manifest. Think to yourself, "Reset!" and then purposefully notice how you are succeeding or reflecting a great quality in the next moment.

   If you like, use your creativity (another great quality) to come up with your own way of resetting. You can simply think with clarity: "Stop" or "Chill." Or, try the version created by Nurtured Heart therapist and trainer Lisa Bravo: "Bless and release." Find a version that works to divert that energetic stream away from the negative and to the positive. Consciously capture the energy of negative emotion as fuel for the fire of positivity.

4. **Engage the reset most strongly when problems rear their heads.** Let's

say that you get into an argument over an important issue. Instead of attacking, retreating or defending, reset yourself to see greatness in the moment. You might say to the other person, "I see you're passionate about this issue and I respect your willingness to talk it over with me." If you are handling strong emotions well, acknowledge yourself for this, too.

5. **Find a way in which you are already reflecting the qualities you most wish you possessed.** Let's say you wish to be more balanced. Rather than saying to yourself, "I will be more balanced," or "I'm so out of balance," *seek out ways in which you already are reflecting this quality.* "I'm juggling work and self-care beautifully by making it to the gym three days a week even though things are pretty stressed these days. I am the greatness of balance."

Fling wide your doors of self-perception and allow yourself to notice ever-expanding horizons of your own great qualities and those of others. Refer back to the list of Qualities and Values Worth Acknowledging (Chapter 4) and the list of emotions (Chapter 5) and practice seeing how your choices reflect those qualities. Recognize yourself for dealing well with emotions.

As you explore those lists, begin to play around with them as *qualities of greatness*—natural outgrowths of the intrinsic, undeniable greatness that every person possesses. Try saying silently, "I am the greatness of…" and fill in the quality you are noticing in yourself. To acknowledge the shared greatness of all life, you can even energize your own qualities of greatness in the second person: as you dream up a new way to teach a lesson that will engage your students, you might say to yourself, "We are the greatness of imagination!"

As you shine the light of awareness on these desired qualities in yourself, you cause them to grow. You're watering your garden of greatness instead of the weeds of negativity!

Over time, this practice alters your 'self-talk'—the internal monologue that goes on in your head during nearly every waking hour. Like changing the default setting on a computer, you change your default from worry, misery and doubts (WMDs) to greatness thinking. You transmute their energy to purposefully fuel ever more greatness. It's like adding Miracle Grow to that greatness garden.

When evidence of your own greatness is presented to you either by yourself or by someone else, take a moment to stand in your greatness and breathe it in. You can try actually breathing it into your heart center (the very middle of your chest, over your sternum) with one long, slow, deep breath. It may prove difficult to prevent a genuine smile from spreading across your face while you stand in greatness.

When I am really conscious about the beauty of this process, I'll even take the random "good job" or "thank you" that comes my way and internally translate it to what that person *intended* to say—what they'd say if they could "talk greatness." Taking generous liberties in this regard builds inner wealth like nobody's business…and it's fun!

Using the Greatness Practice in Relationships

In an e-mail, principal Karen Calkins shared with me how the approach was changing not only the relationships between Cooley Middle School students and educators, but between the administrators and teachers:

> *A new challenge for me has been to apply the principles of the approach to difficult teachers….We refuse to energize negativity and hold ourselves to utilizing the approach with difficult teachers just as sincerely as we would with one of our students. Miraculous things are happening!*

Do you have colleagues, friends or family members who seem to love to dish out negativity to you? Most of us have at least one person like this in our lives. Greatness practice can work wonders to shift this dynamic between spouses, co-workers and adult family members. And you don't have to make any effort at all to change the other person—it's all about changing your own response to the negativity that's coming your way.

Let's say someone is dishing negativity your way, and you feel a strong emotion such as anger, sadness, frustration or annoyance. You feel it. You take it in. Your urge is probably to dish it right back. Instead, reset and think to yourself, *No thank you.* Dig down deep and find some greatness to reflect back to the other person; you are handing that negative energy back on a positive platter by pointing out that greatness.

Relationships between adults tend to become alive and vibrant mainly in response to problems. Deep conversation and intimacy often arise when complaints or problems are being discussed; relationships can grow and deepen through shared negativity. If you have a desire to shift this, the next time someone tries to engage you in relationship around problems, ask him or her what's going right, or point out what *you* see that's great right now.

For example, let's say a co-worker is complaining about a difficult student's most recent successful attempt to derail her classroom. You might once have said something like, "Oh, man, *that* kid is a handful. What did you do next?" Or, "His parents must have forgotten to give him his meds this morning." Or you might have tried to offer some helpful advice about how to solve her problem, which many might see as a *positive* response. But even giving advice ends up fueling the flames of problem orientation. It suggests to the other person that she isn't capable of solving her own problem.

In contrast, choose positivity. You can begin your response with great compassion: "First of all, I really get how much you care. You so want this child to succeed and you are trying so hard to find solutions. You are being resourceful." And then turn the negatives into positives by asking, "What did he do right today? What rules were not broken? Tell me what else went well in your classroom."

If she tries to go back to problems, you have two main choices. The first is to keep refusing to energize her negativity and resolving to energize the positive. I am surprised at how well people react when I simply state, "I'm not going to go there with you, but I will talk about what went right. I know you are a great teacher who is making great effort with great intention." The shift to what's right typically happens quite smoothly from there. (This way of steering the conversation to what's going right works beautifully in administrative and faculty meetings, too.)

In consultations with me about their children or students, folks often want desperately to talk about issues and problems. They want to get right down to the nitty-gritty of what's going wrong. I stop them as soon as I detect that the tenor of the energy is negative. I tell them that I can only help them if I know how the approach is taking hold. So I kindly ask how it's going in terms of energizing success. How does it feel to them? How are the children responding? As we explore this in some detail, I usually get plenty to applaud and appreciate. Then I'll ask how it's going with refusing to give energy to negativity, and again, there's usually so much to applaud and appreciate. Finally, I ask how they're doing with the Stand of clarity and limit setting.

Often, the person has forgotten what the original issues were by the time we've applauded and appreciated all these unfolding successes. Now we have relationship based on a positive and acknowledging energy that's so much sweeter and more productive than any conversation we could have had about problems. Now there's truly a way forward: we can notch up what's already working well.

If I don't want to have internal relationship with myself based on a flow of negative energy, why would I want to have relationships with others based on it? So many therapists get worn out physically and emotionally from exposure to that energy day in and out. You couldn't pay me enough to take that on. In my estimation, it's far more compassionate to take good care of yourself while aiding and abetting a positive direction with others. We aren't demonstrating compassion when we give warnings to boundary-pushing children; nor are we being compassionate when we choose to facilitate and feed into exchanges that revolve around complaints, worries, misery or doubt.

The second choice you have with that complaining colleague who, despite your firmness in your three Stands, seems bent on reverting back to negativity, is to give her what amounts to a reset by changing the subject or politely exiting the conversation.

Resetting Other Adults

You can reset anyone who tries to take you down the road of negativity by calmly, un-energetically removing your energy from the equation. There's nothing punitive or rude about it. I've been known to reset people at my trainings for asking off-topic or off-purpose questions! (I recommend doing this with students, too, once you have this approach up and running in your class.) Although for an adult, being reset in public might seem humiliating, these people usually thank me later on. They often tell me that the reset led to beneficial insight into old patterns. Sometimes, they add that they now feel they have permission to internally say 'no' to intruding, disruptive thoughts—permission they apparently never thought they had.

The greatness practice is *not* about just being sweet and nice and never hashing out difficult problems or relationships. We all have to do this at times at work and at home. Your emotions during difficult times are strong fuel for greatness, too. "I am feeling so angry right now about an injustice, and I'm choosing to keep my cool and express it cleanly and directly to the person with whom I have an issue." Or, "I'm feeling so sad because I miss my sister. I'm letting myself really feel this and not trying to distract myself or use substances to feel better. I am the greatness of honest emotion."

If we keep our eyes on the prize of positivity, of greatness, we don't get mired down in negativity as we work through our processes with each other. We can stay clearer about what we believe, what we need and where we want to end up in any situation. And problems have a way of solving themselves when you refuse to energize them and go to greatness instead.

The Gift of the Reset, Revisited

Going 'offline' from greatness does have a benefit, however: when we've reset back online to the greatness of ourselves and others, we see that glory as though it's new. We're further inspired to stay online and to upgrade to the newest, fastest version! The more we reset ourselves, the better we come to know when we need to reset and reboot to be back to where we want to be. We can move through this with the same ease of a computer that's set up to do these things automatically. We come to recognize that our work is at a standstill when we're bumped offline. It is when we are online to that greatness place that our best work gets done and our best lives get lived.

Notching it Up!

Nurtured Heart Fearlessness

When people first learn this approach—sometimes, even before they actually try it—a lot of fear arises. They intuitively see how and why it works. They might even have the "aha moment" where they see how standard modes of discipline are upside-down and how the methods of this approach turn them right-side-up. But then, the "what if" questions pop up.

"What if a child won't do a reset?"

"What if a child won't comply with any request?"

"What if I don't do the positive reflections correctly?"

"What if I can't come up with the right words?"

"What if a child laughs at or insults me?"

"What if a child hurts another child or destroys property or just threatens to do that?"

"What if I get so emotionally wound up that I can't do the approach?"

Hopefully, by this point in this book, you can figure out how you might deal with these specific situations. But the truth is that things will come up that you never even dreamed of—really, isn't that how life is in general? Rather than trying to prepare for every eventuality with a game plan, I advise you to be *absolutely fearless.*

Fearlessness in the Nurtured Heart Approach takes form as:

- Refusing to energize negativity
- Refusing to forget to relentlessly energize success
- Confronting the success of rules not broken
- Not needing to know why; just giving resets and getting back to time-in
- Refusing to give warnings
- Believing that intensity and life force are gifts
- Not turning to diagnoses, evaluations or psychiatric meds if at all possible
- Willingness to let go of any conflicting advice
- Willingness to use the approach for all children

- Attributing great intention to parents, teachers and children
- Fearlessly using WMD energy to fuel greatness; purposefully re-setting to greatness

This doesn't mean fears won't surface within you. But you can use that energy to propel greatness. Personally, I often privately use any intense emotion to push my dedication to and intention toward greatness beyond any prior limitations. When I'm fearful because of a personal moment of anguish or news of some tragedy, I purposely allow myself to feel this fear or anguish as deeply and efficiently as possible. I feel it consciously and fearlessly, right square in my heart. But then, in a matter of moments, I pulsate that same great emotional energy into my next iterations of exploring greatness.

Chapter 10
Summary

Key Concepts

- What children want from adults, most of all, is connected, energized and intense relationship.

- When children behave well, they generally get little energy from us; when they act out, break rules or threaten to break rules, they get large-scale evidence of energy, connection and relationship. Unfortunately, the child's translation of this is that he gets the most love and intimacy through negativity and poor choices.

- Although what the child receives for poor behavior might be negative in tenor (punishment, lecture, warnings), the child still is fed energetically by the interaction. The child feels plugged into a super-connected broadband, so to speak, through negativity. And some children can't help but go back for more—particularly when interactions remain low-key, disconnected and unanimated while they are not acting out. Compared to the higher connectivity from negative behavior, the positives they receive feel like dial-up!

- The more intense the child, the more willing the child is to get that relationship for negativity.

- Normal methods typically learned by educators for dealing with rule-breaking in the classroom give even more energy when children are doing things wrong. This is why normal, conventional methods tend to make difficult children's boundary-pushing behavior worse rather than better.

The Three Stands

Stand 1: Refuse to energize negativity (absolutely NO!): Don't get drawn in by a child's problems; make the response to acting-out and rule-breaking predictably boring.

Stand 2: Relentlessly energize success (absolutely YES!): Use the approach's four techniques to find and verbally comment upon successes small, large and in between, focusing on how the child's everyday actions incontrovertibly demonstrate that he or she is successful and possesses greatness. This is the state of being we call "time-in," when all is well and problems are not happening.

Active Recognition: Seeing and acknowledging with detail and without judgment, as though describing the scene to a blind person.

"Tim, I see that you're putting purple and yellow stripes around the edges of your chalk drawing."

"Patty, Olivia, Theresa, and Eddie, I see you carefully putting your books into your backpacks and being very organized with your paperwork."

Experiential Recognition: Adding to Active Recognitions examples of values or qualities lived and expressed in the moment, essentially shining the light on the child's embodiment of them—and the greatness this reflects.

"Yolanda, I see that you've chosen to read during free time instead of playing a game. I admire your desire to keep increasing your knowledge right now—that's a great expression of curiosity and diligence."

"This whole half of the room is paying such close attention to this lesson. I can see how intensely you are concentrating. You have the greatness of focus and discipline."

"Rafael, I see that you're not happy with your collage art and that you're getting a fresh piece of paper so you can start a new one. You handled your displeasure so well—letting go of the one you didn't like and starting over shows me how you value getting it just the way you like it, even if it means a little extra work. That's determination!"

Proactive Recognition: Teaching rules by freely giving recognition of rules followed.

"Jordan, I see you're feeling really frustrated right now—you're clenching your hands and frowning, and you look like you want to kick the leg of your desk...but you aren't. That's using great control."

"Tanya, you could have gotten out of your seat when you had your hand up for a while and I didn't call on you. But you didn't. Thanks for being patient while I finished with my other tasks."

"Manny, I can see that you are sad about not being able to go to the computer lab with the first group. I also see that you're not arguing, pushing anyone or trying to sneak out without my noticing. You're showing me awesome self-control right now."

"Noelle, Jack, and Ivan, you guys are sitting so close in your work group but you aren't talking—you're just getting your own worksheets done. That's a great demonstration of calm and clear intention. It shows me your great purpose."

Creative Recognition: Creatively 'hijacking' challenging students into moments of compliance and success—do whatever it takes to give the child an experience of success.

While Frank throws his waste papers into the recycling bin: "Frank, I have to accuse you of being responsible. You chose to toss your papers into the recycle bin instead of leaving them on the floor or tossing them into the trash, where they wouldn't get recycled. You somehow knew intuitively that I was wanting that to get done, and you took the appropriate action. Trusting your intuition and taking action are great qualities that you have."

While Gretchen is standing near you at the whiteboard: "Here, Gretchen, hold this," as you hand her the eraser. "Wow, Gretchen, thanks for helping out with the eraser! You were right there when I needed you." As she starts to erase the board: "I need you to erase the board for me…Whoa! Did you read my mind? Your helpfulness is really shining forth today."

Stand 3: Clearly but un-energetically enforce limits. Be free of confusion and ambiguity about rules and rigorous in regard to consequences (absolutely clear!). State rules in their negative version (with the word "no") for absolute clarity and make it your mission to teach these rules by applauding children when rules are not being broken. Do not give warnings or other energy to negativity when a rule is broken. Instead, deliver an un-energized, unceremonious time-out/reset every time a rule is broken. Then it's back to time-in. Keep the line between time-in and time-out perfectly clear, as it is in a **video game** or sporting event. Students need to really feel the difference for the approach to work. Time-out/reset is not a punishment; it's an opportunity for the child to get herself back on track in the next "now," where rules are not being broken.

Remember the cadence of the dance of greatness: the primal rhythm of what you have set out to do and the basis of any journey. It's left foot, then right foot—curriculum, then recognitions, then back to curriculum.

A Brief Review of the Nurtured Heart Time-Out/Reset

Resets should:

- Be as short as possible (two seconds to one minute)
- Be as unceremonious and as un-energized as possible
- Bring the student back to time-in by first congratulating him for completing the reset and then recognizing something he is doing right.
- Be given as often as needed in response to rules broken
- Take place in the classroom, preferably in the student's seat

- Be given in tandem with continuing to hand out positives to the rest of the room
- Be applied to one's self when necessary in order to maintain the first Stand

Epilogue

You've reached the end of the journey that is this book. Your perseverance in reading this far and doing your best to take its concepts and advice to heart speak volumes about your willingness to learn, your devotion to doing your job well, and your dedication to helping as many of your students as possible benefit from their time in your classroom. I applaud your greatness.

Work with this approach, notch it up as needed and explore the possibilities in a way that sings for you. A thousand educators will manifest the elements of this approach in a thousand different ways.

My vision is that, in this independent spirit of empowerment, you will carry this out in ways that will address the most challenging children and the most challenging scenarios.

You now have everything you need to make that happen—to essentially become the approach. Congratulations!

Left foot. Right foot.

Resources

Nurtured Heart Approach Support Information

Three web sites are available to those who seek further information about the Nurtured Heart Approach:

www.DifficultChild.com
www.ChildrensSuccessFoundation.com
www.NurturingGreatness.net

The first site, DifficultChild.com, is designed to be a resource for the Nurtured Heart Approach. Anyone can sign up to be on the mailing list and receive a great summary of *10 Ways to Propel Your Challenging Child to Greatness*. Also by signing up, you will receive Nurtured Heart newsletters with updates related to the approach, special offers and special notices. EnergyParenting.com is the online learning center for the Nurtured Heart Approach. It is a members-only website where parents, educators, coaches and therapists gain quick acquisition of the approach techniques and then continually hone their expertise through innovative learning modules, discussion forums, tele-seminars as well as feature articles, products and services supporting the approach. Readers can join EnergyParenting.com at a special reduced rate by sending an e-mail to susan@EnergyParenting.com with the subject line "I want the friends of Howard Glasser offer."

All three web sites listed above have research findings related to this work, information about coaching and therapy services, information about ongoing workshops and Advanced Trainings, and information about creating training events for your organization.

Books on the Nurtured Heart Approach

Those listed below are available in most libraries and bookstores and from online sources. They can also be ordered at the Nurtured Heart Approach web sites DifficultChild.com or NurturingGreatness.net, or via a toll-free call to 800-311-3132.

- *Transforming the Difficult Child: The Nurtured Heart Approach* (Revised 2008) by Howard Glasser and Jennifer Easley

- *All Children Flourishing – Igniting the Greatness of Our Children* (2008) by Howard Glasser with Melissa Lynn Block.

- *Transforming the Difficult Child Workbook – An Interactive Guide to the*

Nurtured Heart Approach (2008) by Howard Glasser, Joann Bowdidge and Lisa Bravo.

- *The Inner Wealth Initiative – The Nurtured Heart Approach for Educators* (2007) by Howard Glasser and Tom Grove with Melissa Lynn Block.

- *You Are Oprah – Igniting the Fires of Greatness* (2009) by Howard Glasser with Melissa Lynn Block

- *ADHD Without Drugs – A Guide to the Natural Care of Children with ADHD* (2010) by Sanford Newmark, M.D.

- *Transforming the Difficult Child: True Stories of Triumph* (2008) by Jennifer Easley and Howard Glasser

- *101 Reasons to Avoid Ritalin Like the Plague Including One Great Reason Why it's Almost Always Unnecessary* (2005) by Howard Glasser

Audio Visual

Transforming the Difficult Child: The Nurtured Heart Approach training tapes are available on CD (audio only, 2.5 hours); on audiotape (2.5 hours); and on DVD (audio-visual with 6-hour and 4-hour versions). All of these can be ordered via the web sites and toll-free number listed above.

Transforming the Difficult Child: The Nurtured Heart Approach – Audio Book (2012) – by Howard Glasser and Jennifer Easley, read by Howard Glasser.